Survived By

A Memoir in Verse + Other Poems

Anne Marie Wells

For my father, "The Big Dipper"

Terry R. Wells

February 11, 1945 - February 6, 2020

Table of Contents

These lines helped me survive. Do what you need with them to survive too. Draw on these pages. Or tear them out. Carry a poem in your pocket. Or give it to someone else. Cross out my words and write your own. Make a collage. Use them as kindling.

Just show me what you create.

@AnneMarieWellsWriter
AnneMarieWellsWriter.com

September

Where is the How-To Guide for tragedy? The textbook
for Grief 101? *What to Expect When You're Expecting
Someone You Love to Die?* How do people learn what to do
when their father has stage 4 lung cancer?

Have experts established scientifically proven steps? Perhaps

> *Step 1: Stop breathing as electric burning emanates outward
>   from your sternum.*
>
> *Step 2: Feel as if seashells have been placed over your ears.*
>
> *Step 3: Tremble like a rescue dog on the Fourth of July*

> *If you've made it to Step 3, good job!   You're doing great!*

> *This is your life now.*

The night my mom calls to tell me

The News

I have plans. A Tinder date with a guy who is totally… fine.
Supposed to go to my friend's art gallery opening, but
I haven't received any confirmation from him.
Even though I'm still on the phone with my mom,
I send him a text—which I still find, to this day, to be very generous.

> *Hey. I don't know if you were planning on going to the
> opening or not, but I'm not going to make it. I just found out
> my dad has terminal lung cancer, and, just to be transparent, I
> was already totally dead on the inside. Now, I'm even deader,
> which I didn't think was possible. Anyway, I don't have the
> capacity to make out with someone on a regular basis right
> now. Take care.*

He calls me.
I hate when strangers call me, and he is still
a stranger. I am still a stranger. He's known me
for two—maybe three—weeks, so there's no way
for him to know I hate when strangers call...
or that I think we're strangers, even though we kissed
once—or was it twice?—or for him to know
anything
about me.

I decline the call.
He leaves a voicemail.

I hate when people leave voicemails—strangers or not.
My voicemail message specifically says,

> *Please hang up and send me an email or a text.*

Before I hang up with Mom, I try to ask her

> *What should I do?*

The words can't wrestle themselves out
from the weight of my wails.

Honey, I can't understand you. Say it again.

> My mom sounds as if this is a normal
> conversation about my work or the dogs
> or the latest hurricane to bronco toward the east coast.

> > *Should I come home?*
> > I say louder, taking my time
> > to cradle each word in my mouth,
> > to roll each letter around my tongue
> > like a lozenge.

Sure. You can come home whenever you want.
Her tone still sounds like she is responding to

Hey, I have nothing better to do,
would it be okay
if I come home for a visit?

And not
Should I come home
to be with Dad
before he dies?

No! No! No!

Frustration barrels out from the pit
in my stomach. She isn't understanding,
or is pretending not to.

Should I come home
to be with you guys? If
it's going to be six months, I'll quit
my job, sell my things, leave Wyoming.
I'll come to Florida and be with you.
But if it's going to be five years—

Honey.

Mom interrupts, and I hear the strain
in the clench of her molars.

It's not going to be five years, Honey.

I can't breathe.
Burning chest.
Seashell ears.
Rescue dog knees.
I have a new life

I never expected to have.

Naive. Or delusional. Everyone loses
their parents, or their parents lose them first. Everyone
experiences loss.
But I wasn't supposed to.

I listen to Tinder Guy's voicemail after I say
goodbye to my mom.

> *Hi, Anne Marie. Yeah, long day. I'm sorry to hear about your*
> *father. That's obviously shitty. So, I'm not sure how you're*
> *feeling in general. I got your text. Yeah, whatever. No*
> *worries. But give me a call when you have a few. I'd like to*
> *talk. Take care.*

I hate him.
I send another text.
      I still regret it.

> *Hey. You are nice and funny and handsome,*
> *and I mean this as nicely as I can:*
> *Please go away.*

He responds:

> *?*
> *You're going to have to rephrase that.*

      I block his number.

He is a perfectly fine person, and I'm sure
he only wants me to be kinder to him, but
and I cannot
give a fuck
about his feelings when
my bones are liquefying into acid, rotting

my organs, my muscles from the inside out.

I text Bert.

Bert's real name is Robert. I call him Bert.
Only I
call him Bert.
And he didn't even like it
in the beginning. (Maybe still doesn't.)
I called him Bert anyway, call him Bert anyway
because I liked it, because I like it, liked
to feel different, special
because he was different, special
to me.

We dated before, but he wanted too much
too soon, and I startle easily. Like a cat rescued
from the pound, I will not go near a kennel
without spitting and drawing blood. But he kept
leaving cans of tuna on the porch, and I kept
coming back, avoiding his touch, scurrying away
if he tried to get too close again.

Would you want to come hang out with me while I sob?

He has no reason to say yes,
but I have nothing to lose.
Not even shame.

I'll be there in a minute.

Maybe I'll elope with him in a hot air balloon one day.

I'm lying in bed with Bert
watching *Harry Potter and the Goblet of Fire*, hating
existence, hating everyone, hating even Bert.
I am a fearful person, not a hateful person,
normally. Before.

Maybe this is me now. Under the shadow of impending loss.

A person who feels contempt
toward those who show her love,
even toward Bert
who deserves someone who can love him back
and doesn't deserve to be hated just for living,
for breathing—without any effort—especially when I asked him
if he would breathe next to me—the louder the better,
who brought my favorite snacks with him—nothing
that requires cooking.

He knows how I hate cooking.

How could I be so full
of rage toward this gentle man
who has done nothing,

nothing,

to hurt me—
not even unintentionally?

I'm waiting for my Advil PM to kick in
watching Voldemort kill Cedric Diggory.
Despite being dead on the inside and despite
my illogical, temporary hatred of Bert, I'm grateful
I'm not alone. I'm grateful Bert either cares
about me this much even when I am
a living nightmare or he is also
so hollowed out
by loneliness
that even filling
the emptiness
with me
will do.

Maybe both. Two things can be true
at the same time, after all.
        And if two things can be true at the same time,

can't I be both
grateful to not be alone
and to have Bert breathing
next to me
at the same time as
being full of anger and resentment
toward every human being
including him?

Perhaps, then:

*Step 1: Skip Denial, go straight to the Anger stage
of grief.*

Step 2: Not just Anger, but Fury. Rage. Wrath.

Step 3: Become paralyzed with bitterness.

The next day, Sadie shows up at my house
unannounced. I thought I hated
When people turned up at my house
unannounced, but like with voicemails, maybe
it's only when strangers turn up
unannounced
that I hate it.

Sadie isn't a stranger.
She's nearly a decade younger than I am, but full
of the kind of wisdom that sits in the mind of a person
four times her age, wisdom that often goes ignored because
she wears floral, summer dresses, and not pant suits, because
she's a barista and not a barrister, because
she says "like," "um," and "you know," and ends
declarative sentences with question marks, and because
she is a woman in her twenties.

She has a bag of ready-to-eat groceries with her.
    Like Bert,
    she knows I hate cooking.

             The other day, I took a picture of a spider
             living in a web on my stovetop—
             the other day
             when I could laugh at myself still,
             when I could laugh
             at all
             still.

Last year, Sadie lost her brother in the middle of the night
as he slept. Twenty-one. No drugs. No alcohol. No known cause.

             No closure.

Her best friend. Her person.
Kidnapped by death.
Truly stolen from her world without warning.

When It happened, I read
all of her blog posts
chronicling her grief. I read
articles and watched
videos about how to care for someone living
through loss. Was I studying
for a test I didn't know I was going to take?

Last year, I bought her family ready-to-eat meals
from the supermarket, signed a bereavement card.
A year later, she's bringing me frozen pizza,
toaster waffles, and ingredients for smoothies.

Sadie sits with me on my sofa.
Listens to me cry. Cries
herself.
Listens to me scream. Screams

herself.
She tells me
of her journey to rebuild
her bones
after death detonated an atomic bomb
in the center of her world.
I decide,
in that moment,
the only people I want to talk to
are those who have had their core sliced, carved
like a Christmas ham.

Sadie leaves, and I call my mom
to hear what the update is, if
my dad has left the hospital yet.

I expect to hear her crisp Hello
but am greeted by my father's voice.
What's left of it.

Each word is a whisper with an extra gasp of air
to give the syllables enough force to exit his mouth.

>*Hello?*
>His voice, small like a votive's light,
>has the same sing-songy intonation it has always had.

>>>>*Hi, Daddy.*

>>>>My knees fold beneath my weight
>>>>as if they're suddenly made of paper.
>>>>I slide to the floor
>>>>unable to even make it to a chair.

>*How ya' doin?*
>he asks as if it were any other day, any other
>life—

as if his throat wasn't clawing for air.

I'm awful!

My words garble,
my face contorts,
a gargoyle
channeling tears
away from my chin

I'm awful!

I mouth it again,
inarticulate.
I want to shout it
loud enough for him to hear
the vehemence.

Do you hear me?
I'm awful! AWFUL!

But only the moans
of a terrified daughter
resound.

It's not that bad,
he wheezes.

It's not that bad?
What the fuck is he talking about?
It's not that bad?

This isn't sad. I'm old.
I'm old. I've had a good life.

My dad is almost 75.
He smoked cigars for 30 years,
and when he ended up in the hospital
with his blood oxygen levels in the 70s,

needing machines to help him breathe,
I knew.
>   We all did.

But the official Bad News came five weeks later
on September 13th, a Friday.

I can't stop envisioning the high school track
across the street from the house where I grew up.
Dad walked laps there at night
with his cigar.
If my sister and I walked over to meet him, we'd know
where he was based on the glowing red ember
bobbing in the dark.

This seemed so normal to us then.
A middle-aged man power-walking,
sneakers tied,
sweatpants, t-shirt, sweatband
around his forehead,
puffing away
at a cigar
the whole time he was getting in his cardio.

We bought him cigars

>   for his birthday.
>   And Christmas.
>   And Father's Day.

And now, he will never walk me down the aisle.
>   My future kids won't know what it is
>   to be loved by their grandfather.
>   To be held in his arms. To
>   sit on his shoulders. To
>   hear his jokes, his stories, his wisdom.

Mom emails me a picture of Dad
to show me how good he looks. How he's doing
fine.

I see my grandparents' faces in his.

We were supposed to go on a family vacation.
We started planning, started saving.
Now, I'm selling my belongings. Making arrangements
to work remotely. Receiving reminders to cherish
every moment. I'm asking people for their advice,
then upon receiving it,
I restrain my frothing screams.

Fuck you and your goddamn fucking advice,
you cancer-free assholes!

How badly my tongue wants to spit
a torrent of resentment
at every Tinder date past and present, every
ex-lover who couldn't properly love me, every
ex-lover *I* couldn't properly love, every
friend who was no longer my friend,
anyone who had ever done me wrong,
even every acquaintance, every colleague,
every well-meaning friend who has done nothing
to hurt me, even my good friends
who *I* called to sob to, who *listened*
to my sobs, who were kind
and wonderful—just everyone,
even my dog—no not my dog, actually—
but everyone else,
even the people I truly, deeply love, even *myself*—
Please, just

Fuck.
Off.

So maybe *that's* Step 1.

Step 1: Fuck off.

The tumors spread
across the maps of his lungs
like spider webs caught in a rainforest, a mother fighting
to protect her young in the pouring tempest, digging her fronds
into his chest, branches cinched in a silken corset, a legacy
at risk with each gust, rigging a gridiron
of wind and leaves the night
of Friday the Thirteenth.

No Unknowing

Eta Canis Minoris

A Ribcage
After Athena Liu

We find our own meaning through the stories we tell
[our]
selves. Our brains swear we live between two carved years, our
[hearts]
insisted from the beginning that this is a
[lie]
passed on for centuries. We must propound the words
[splayed]
on ossified elements into existence
[like]
a child's make-believe world. We can—must— will ourselves
[wild]
like Holocene beasts. Rid ourselves of time like the
[dogs]
who learned to croon in the key of Canis Minor
[had]
done ages ago. I don't know what's true and what's
[a]
fairy tale letting me feel settled, stable or
[free]
from dying, but I choose settled, stable, and free
[for]
now, since I've never been quite sure what's true after
[all.]

Am I still a child
playing in the chapel pews
missing the message?

All you will have is your resentment
packed in a suitcase,
your hungry dog
on a leash when you ask
the Universe,

           Am I a bad person?

She will not respond,
you will keep talking.

        I think I must be a bad person
           because people only go out
              of their way to fuck over
                bad people.

...

…

        Is that why this is happening to me?

The Universe will give you a glance,
red lip, eyebrow raised, then she'll ask,

Who are you?

It's Not Personal

Cast iron sky, seals
a chlorophyll tunnel,

corn stalks waving hello
as they whisper so long.

Squint, hypnotized
by honey dashes,

daydreaming of the prayers
each ear sends into the ether,

if they might, if I asked,
use their spears as steeples,

form an acres-large
congregation to build

a miracle out of

Meager Material

One Week Later

It is easy for me to be honest, to be
straightforward about my feelings, especially if asked
a direct question   (not of the romantic variety).

It is easy for me to give compliments, to provide
words of affirmation
when they are due.
It is easy for me to set boundaries
or to ask for help.
It is easy for me to complain
or to give my honest opinion   (when asked for it).
It is harder for me, in fact,
to keep my feelings inside.

My sister and I mirror
each other in this way
sometimes.

> We are best friends even though
> I live in the Teton Mountains, and she
> in the D.C. suburbs.
>
> One of my favorite memories of her is when
> she called me to say,

> > *I'm about to do one of my favorite things.*
> > > *Play Scrabble?*
> >
> > *No.*
> > > *Make a spreadsheet?*
> >
> > *No.*
> > > *What is it?*
> > *I'm about to write a letter of complaint.*

I know many people who suffer

in silence. They will tolerate anything or anyone
to be a good sport, to not disrupt, to not be

> a nuisance.

My dad,
if you ask him,

> *What do you think about Todd?*

and he thinks Todd is a real "*Jerk with a capital A,*"
as we say in our family,
my dad will pause.
After taking a breath, he'll say

> *... Todd's okay.*

My dad embodies Robert Brault's quote,

> *Today I bent the truth to be kind...*
> *for I am far surer of what is kind*
> *than I am of what is true.*

We all want to help him, and he says,

Am I happy? Am I asking for help?

> *Well, no, you're not asking for help,*
> *but I don't think you would ask for it*
> *even if you wanted it!*

My father and I are both the youngest-born children
in our families. In a way I was raised with three parents,
my older sister always wanting to mother me
instead of sister me.

I wonder if my uncle tried to father my father
instead of brother him.

I wonder if my petulant complaints growing up rang familiar
to my father's ears from his own upbringing:

> *I can do it myself!*
> *I don't need help!*
> *Leave me alone!*

When I tell Mom I'll be driving out
to Florida with Bert and Bella Bird
in October to help care for Dad, she asks,
What? Like for a couple of weeks?

> Um. No. Not for a couple of weeks.

> *Hi, Dad!*
> *Yes, I'm uprooting my entire life*
> *in order to move in with you*
> *and live with you indefinitely!*
> *I know you didn't ask for this,*
> *but this is your/my new life now!*
> *Sorry, not sorry!*

I don't understand   (when I need it)
not asking for help
because I did not inherit
the don't-be-a-nuisance DNA.

No one ever has to guess
if I'm happy
or not.
They will know
by the confetti cloud of cartoon hearts
billowing from my eyes as I pirouette
through the air like a Monarch
on its migratory journey home, or if not
I will engulf them in my molten lava,

envelope them like a fire god's wrath
on a village that did not perform
their yearly ritual to keep me
from wreaking havoc on their crops.

They will know.
I will tell them—

even if it's inconvenient.

News flash: I am suffering!
And my suffering   *is*
consuming me!

I want everyone to know!
Hey! Does everyone know I am suffering?   *Hey, you!*
Do you know?

Do you know that my dad
is going to die,
and I am suffering?

No, no, no, **he's** *not*
suffering!

I'm *suffering!*

You didn't know? Well, I am!
How about you, over there?   *Did*
you know?

Hey! Stop walking away from me!

I am trying to tell
You how much I am
suffering!

When I'm sad, it is hard for me
to keep it in, even harder
for me to not do everything in my power
to make myself
sadder.

I don't know why

I do this,
but I do.

When I got

The News

my mind went straight to who and what
I don't have in my life.   (Mostly who.)
Like my ex, AJ.
Our sparring words have long died and seeped
into the soil, overtaken by mushrooms and earthworms, and still
he would never have sat with me while I sobbed, would never
have brought me groceries, would never have held me in his arms
through the night just to be there for me,
if sex weren't on the table   (or the couch or the floor)
even if I asked him outright if he would comfort me—
                especially if asked him outright.

For the brief time we were involved, anything I asked
was interpreted as making demands.
Maybe this is what happens
when one self-absorbed idiot dates another.

And I know if I were to ask him
to be here
for me now,
to just sit with me
while I sobbed
about my father
dying,
he would,
like he always has,
in so many words,
say no.

The week before my dad's diagnosis,

when I thought I was going through a hard time *then*,
after Bella Bird broke her leg playing fetch,
I asked him if he could come be with me
when I wanted the comfort of a familiar voice,
familiar scents and fingertips, the heartbeat
of someone I (used to) love, someone Bella loved.
He said no.
He says no
every time.
He said no
even when we were together.
Like watching the tragic
scene of a 1990s drama.
No matter how many times I watch,
the same bitter ending repeats itself.
It's almost as if I keep rewatching
just to prove myself right.
And if I consult with my Wise Mind,
it will affirm that his *no* is actually… a gift.

Replete with the kind of on-again-off-again turmoil
inherent with two people whose only common interests
lay between the fitted sheet and duvet, I'm not sure why I thought
perhaps after having split up
we'd forge a friendship of laughter
and meaningful conversation,
vulnerability and understanding.

I don't judge him for saying no.　　　　(...Maybe that's a lie.)
I don't *want* to judge him for saying no.
Maybe my Logical Mind understands
and my Emotional Mind still holds it against him.

My Logical Mind knows
he owes me nothing,　　(He's made it very clear.)
knows he has no reason to be present for me

other than empathy   (Which he has also made very clear
                            he doesn't owe me either.)
These are just facts.
But my Emotional Mind takes over
the facts and wrenches the bolts on my heart
a little bit tighter.

I wish I could go back in time
to my life before
                            The News.

Before my eyes would seek the arms
on the clock like a tic just to calculate

> *A few minutes ago, my life was different.*
> *An hour ago, I didn't know.*
> *Twenty-four hours ago, I had no idea*
> *my life was about to change forever.*

Friday, one week later, I have a moment
of normality when I first wake up. Just a moment.
A single moment
before remembering.
                    At this time a week ago, I still didn't know.
For the rest of my life,
I will never
not know.
This will never
not be my reality.

I know that instead of focusing
on the people whom I don't have in my life,
I need to focus on the people
I do have.

I ask for help

on social media
even though
I have never entered
any of these friends' homes.
I don't know their birthdays
or middle names. I don't know
their favorite foods, or whether
they're allergic to dogs or peanuts.
But I also don't know
what else to do.
I can't suffer
alone.

I don't know what to do!
I'm in shock and disoriented!
Can anyone help me?

Friends — strangers, loose acquaintances —
say, *Yes! We can help!*

Then ask,
How?

I don't know what to tell them.
I don't mind asking for help, but
I don't like
       strangers.

Well, no.
I like prancing around a room
of familiar and unfamiliar faces,
cutting cake and making toasts,
making the most of any evening
when I curl my hair and put on jewelry.

I do like strangers
               on the surface.

I don't like strangers
>who try to get too close
>too soon.

I need time
to decide if I want someone
around.

Even when I do, I don't return messages
too promptly, don't ask personal questions.
An invisible arm extends from my chest,
palm flexed, fingers spread like five fence posts
that hold the barbed wire taut.

I need time.
>Months!

I get used to a new person
like a gift I didn't ask for.
I don't know what I'm going to do
with them
at first. Sometimes
I throw them out. Sometimes
they get tucked away
on the closet shelf,
>forgotten.

But sometimes,
I question
how I ever lived without them.

When Sadie lost her
will to live
with the loss
of her brother,
all I wanted was to scoop
her in my hand, tend to her
like an injured bird, nurse her
through an out of control situation

that had nothing
to do with me.

How do I anticipate the needs of someone
who is spinning weightless in a tornado of loss and shock
when the wind has never even tussled my hair?

I sent heart emojis
with words that could have filled
the insides
of sympathy cards.

When she didn't respond, I'd take it
as a personal offense.

> *Oh no, I'm overwhelming*
> *her. I'm burdening*
> *her. She doesn't want to hear*
> *from me.*

> *Me, me, me, me, me.*

With that feeling of trying to help
and not knowing how folded
like a to-do list in my front pocket
I respond to people's heart emojis and greeting card words with,

> *I love you so much, but I can't respond right now.*

Yet, most of the time, I still can't
manage to send even that little response. In one moment,
I interact like a well-adjusted human being
with a friend who stops by with a coffee for me, like
a person whose circulatory system hasn't transformed
into a Formula 1 Grand Prix arena, or else
I'm scream-singing along to Lizzo —even as my throat grates
and burns—out my friend's passenger side window.

But I still can't muster a quick *Thanks* to the guy
with good intentions who sends me a text saying,

> *Hope you have been well. I'm really sorry about your father
> and Bella's leg. I know you will be strong for them.*

Maybe I don't want the conversation to continue
after that, and responding,

> *Thanks. Now please go away,*

doesn't feel like the right thing to do.
One friend writes,
I'm so sorry to hear about your dad. Is he in pain?

He has to carry
an oxygen tank
everywhere he goes, and
he's been needled and
threaded and
knifed and
forked and
told he is incurable
and going to die.
Soon.
Not years from now.
Soon.
His shirts that once wrapped
his belly like a tight hug
now hang from his stooped shoulders
as if he were a coat rack.
I'd say that's pretty fucking painful.
If it's not painful for him, it's painful for me, so

fuck off!

Another person asks,
How long does he have?

Answer:

Fuck off.

Responding, particularly to people
I'd like to maintain my intimate distance with, feels like
lighting a campfire while on the lam.

> *But, Anne Marie! Look outside your own pain.*
> *People who you consider strangers, even though*
> *you know their names and faces, want to support you.*
> *Haven't you always ever wanted to be loved?*
> *Love is being handed to you. Take it.*

My friends want to help too, my friends I love and who love me,
the ones whose middle names and birthdays and allergies I know.
But I don't know what to tell any of them.

> *Yes, I'm asking for help.*
> *No, I don't actually know how*
> *anyone can help me.*

> *Do you want to listen to me scream?*

Jessie says *Yes.*
We drive into Grand Teton National Park
with her paddleboard.
She chauffeurs me around String Lake
while I sit cross-legged behind her and yell.

> *It isn't fair my dad has cancer!*

She yells too.

> *No! It isn't fair your dad has cancer! Fuck!*

She listens to me strategize my next steps.
She says,

That's a really great idea.

She never says,
It's going to be okay.

Because, of course, it's not going to be okay.

She just keeps saying,
This isn't fair.
This really fucking sucks.
Fuck!

No. It's not.
Yes. It does.
Fuck, indeed.

Kayla,
my best friend, Kayla, and her partner, Cynthia, live
in New York City. Across the country and across the culture
from me in my rural mountain world.

Kayla is not a stranger.
Her middle name is Danielle.
Her birthday is the day after mine.
She isn't allergic to anything,
but there are plenty of foods she doesn't like.

Kayla and I met in the college dorms.
University at Buffalo. 2007.
Randomly assigned as neighbors
as Fate grinned to herself,
Yes... "randomly"...

Four years later, we recreate *V-J Day in Times Square*
when Governor Cuomo signed the Marriage Equality Act.

Five years later, we cuddle in a double-decker bus

in a snowstorm in London.

Ten years later, we sing Disney songs while leaning against
buck rails lining the Flatirons in Colorado.

She is not a stranger.
When she calls me, I think

Oo! It's Kayla!

and not

Why is this person calling me?

She and Cyn want to "help,"
but what can they possibly do
besides listen to me scream
over the phone?

They buy me a plane ticket to Florida
so I can be with my dad
now.

Before I can drive the three-day journey
from Wyoming to Vero Beach
with Bert and Bella Bird—leaving
the mountains for as long as my dad is alive—
I have to find a subletter and
have my car repaired and
arrange to work remotely.
It takes time. Maybe a month.

Kayla and Cyn's gift is more than just a flight,
it's more time with my dad.
Priceless
time.

I coordinate my connecting flight
with my sister's so that we show up

at the airport at the same time.

My sister already booked her flight;
my parents know she's on her way.
They don't know I'm coming too.

> We have this family expression:
> *What do Wellses love to do?*
>
> The answer is
> *Surprise people.*

More strangers, more loose acquaintances
want to know how they can help.
But I don't want them to listen to me scream.
And I don't want them to buy me flights.
But I don't want them to feel helpless.
And I don't want them to stop asking.

I tell them I hate cooking, and I'll do anything
to not have to exchange pleasantries with people
at a grocery store or restaurant,
people who will ask me,

How are you?
when it's not customary to answer with,

> *I've never experienced a deeper agony*
> *than I currently am,*
> *as if my ribs are made*
> *of double-sided needles*
> *and every inhale, every heartbeat*
> *feels like my organs and flesh are being pricked*
> *by twelve thousand wasps.*

I'd do anything to not have to

brush my hair or change
out of my pajamas.
So, could they please send smoothie ingredients?
And could they please send kibbles for the dog?
But could they please not stay to chat?

They do send smoothie ingredients and kibbles.
And they don't stay to chat.

My dear friends from Colorado
order groceries for me online and have them delivered
to my front doorstep.

My wonderful friend and her husband agree
to stay with Bella Bird while I use my plane ticket gift
to surprise my dad.

A woman I have interacted with only twice—
once at an open house for a yoga studio
and the second time when we both roller skated
in our town's Fourth of July Parade—brings me a box
of fresh fruit, protein powder, aloe extract, green algae,
collagen, maca powder, almond milk, and other odd, lovely things
for smoothies.

Another woman comes to my house
when I'm working late, when I'm not even home.
She brings me three huge containers
of dog food and treats for Bella.

I barely know her.
We met at swing dance night. We never
actually spent time together one-on-one.
She lives forty-five minutes away.
But she still helps.

A woman—a distant acquaintance—who doesn't even live
in Wyoming anymore sends me $10 to help me with expenses.
She just wants to help.

And she does.
Help.
They all.
Help.
It all.
Helps.

Who are these beautiful, kind people
who are going out of their way for me

when I'm so
undeserving?

I keep thinking about all the people
who were supposed to be the ones
bringing me groceries, listening to me scream,
who were supposed to be the ones
to tell me this really fucking sucks,
but who are not,
who are not even sending messages
of condolence or encouragement.
These absent people must know the real me,
must know I don't deserve kindness or care.

> *These present people are only helping me
> because they don't know how awful I really am.*

I can't let them find out.

It's one o'clock in the morning, and my limbs
are puzzle-pieced together with Bert's. Our foreheads touch,
we breathe each other's breath. He's asleep,

and I'm a mess.

I don't deserve you being here.
I deserve to be alone
and sad
and suffering
by myself.

I haven't done anything
to deserve
your support
or your care,
and I can never
pay you back

for what you're doing.

I picture myself as an infant Rhesus monkey
caged in a lab, and Bert as Harry Harlow's
terry-cloth-covered robot. I cling to Bert
for comfort and security, desperate for him
to stay with me so I don't have to face
it all

                              alone.

He takes a moment to fully wake up, to take in
what I blurted out.

> *I didn't have anyone*
> *when my brother died,*
>   *and I wish I did.*
> *You're great,*
> *and it makes me feel good*
> *to be here for you now.*

It takes me a moment to fully take in
his calm, articulate response.

Being with me makes him feel
good
even when I feel
like a shuttered window,
impenetrable to sun, exchanging
vistas for dust and dead flies,

He thinks I'm great
even though I swallow the light
in each room I enter.

He reminds me
providing help
feels good.
If I can accept help,
even if I don't feel like I deserve it,
it actually helps the people around me
who want to feel helpful,
especially when they don't know what to do.

> Like the seeds that grow
> from the dust of another,
> the circle of help
> blossoms into blossoms
> and never ends.

I kiss Bert before walking into the Jackson Hole airport.
When I walk out of the Orlando airport, I stand
next to my sister, waiting for our parents' car to appear.

It's an image I've never seen before:
my mother behind the steering wheel,
but they're laughing. They're laughing.

> Our surprise was a success.

Then we're all laughing. The four of us.
The whole drive back to Vero.

My dad is not dead,
but his death is a looming fact
that is painfully out of place,
like a grain of sand in my eye.

My dad sits in the side room
with his newspaper. Like it's any other day,
any other visit. I follow and sit
next to him.

Dad, you look so thin.

My eyes well, I bite
the inside of my cheeks,
hold my jaw like a carpenter
grips two splinters of wood waiting
for the glue to dry.

He says,
I know, and I can't stop. But I'm eating three meals a day.

If I try to speak, my wooden jaw
will split apart again.
I say nothing.
He keeps talking.

Your mother says I look good.

I say nothing.

*When we first moved into this house,
our neighbor's husband had a stroke
and was bedridden. He died a while later
of cancer and no one knew. No one ever saw him.
So, really, it's not that bad. I'm not bedridden.
That'd be so hard on your mother.*

I'm walking around.
I feel okay.
I don't feel weak.

I say nothing.

I'm happy.
I'm not depressed.
I have a good attitude.

I take that in.

My dad knows he is going to die,
and he has a good attitude about it.

The dam is pried open, my teeth unclench
shards of oak and ash, my eyes unleash eight days of grief.

I do not
have a good attitude.
I do not
have a good anything.

My dad stands and gives me a hug.
I remember lots of hugs hello
and hugs goodbye. I don't remember
hugs of consolation, hugs of comfort.
He'd always been more of a "shake it off"
kind of dad. This hug, his hug, feels
out of the ordinary, but we are already
out of our ordinary. What will ever
be ordinary again?

I'm not strong enough. Dad.

He's so much thinner than I've ever seen him
but still so much bigger and taller than I am.
I always felt so small in his hug. Like a child.

You have to learn to be strong. Seeing you upset
makes me upset, and it'll make your mother upset.
Don't let her see you like this.

> In other words,
> shake it off,
> don't be a nuisance.
> Don't make anyone uncomfortable
> with your pain.
> Don't remind anyone
> of theirs.

Even though death is inevitable
for everyone and everything,
I can't picture the pictures
without him standing beside my mother.
Christmas with only the three of us—
my mother, my sister, and I.
I can't picture visiting
only my mother in Florida,
going to Humiston beach alone,
finding only one perfect seashell
to bring home with me
without my father barefoot, hands clasped
behind his back, looking out into the horizon.
I don't want to picture it,
this new life, a mere shadow
of the life I knew before
7:11 PM on September 13th.
A Friday.
        And the truth is
                I am not strong
enough to tread water in the salty abyss
as I watch the ship sail away.

        I am weak
-hearted. I can't hold my breath for long.

I don't know how to stay afloat
while searching for shallower waters.
I only know how to hope
that my drowning will be quick.

I don't know how to stand my ground
as enemy forces charge at me, swords in hand.
I only know how to curl up in a ball
hoping no one notices my useless body
on the battlefield.

But I'm lucky.
I don't have to know how.
I have an army
of love
covering me in armor, showing me how to thrust a sword,
how to withstand the unseen arrows that will impale me
through the chainmail, to lessen the bleeding, to survive
the battle until it is my time to cause the same kind of grief
in those who love me.

I have a life raft
of love
lashed together by each plank's sorrows, holding me
through the incessant waves soaking my clothes, clawing
at my eyes and mouth. They can't keep me dry, but they can carry
some of my suffering so that I can carry some of my dad's
suffering,
some of my mom's
suffering,
some of my sister's
suffering.

Even if the people surrounding me helping me
carry my suffering aren't the people
I would have originally guessed them to be, even if I don't feel

like I deserve people's kindness, particularly Bert's, I know
I need to accept it because

> I will plummet
> into the sea's silty depths
> without it.

> And

my love army, my life raft need me to accept their help
so that they don't feel helpless, just like I need
my parents to accept my help so that I don't feel helpless.
Breaking the circle of helplessness.

And that lessens the fog of guilt smothering me
when I accept love, kindness, and generosity
I don't feel worthy of.

Step 1: Fuck off.
Step 2: Accept help.

Marilyn en Bleu

Ekphrasis of Sylvestre Gauvrit's sculpture of the same name

I'm Blue like dead lips, like thimble fingertips,
no longer nimble, no longer touch the thumb
one at a time, no longer tremble. I'm Blue

like Patsy Cline, Blue, so lonesome for Blue. Like
myrtille skin peeled, teardrops scaling down its haunch,
yearning to stain *perle*, white teeth *encre*. I'm Blue

like vein-wrapped knuckles, train maps
to ventricles, like bioluminescence *electrique*
under the Cheshire crescent. I'm Blue

like Virgin Mary's Blue veil billowing in the wind
her first time a-wassailin', like dark wash jeans, like
dark wash lungs heaving in denim factories. I am *Bleu*

like the River Seine, its color cigarette ash
dissolved in old gin. What I mean is,
Bleu. Its sound tells you everything. I'm *Bleu*

like the cat eye winking back at Norma Jeane
through the mirror on August 3, 1962, and I wonder,
Madame Monroe, did you wish to be un-*Bleu* too?

A Place in This Universe

i am the ninth
planet or tenth

distant cold
orbit askew

not quite belonging
yet unable to stop

revolving around
a memory of light

Maybe shooting stars
      are nothing but daisy petals
      tossed to the side as
            the Universe wonders
                    whether
                    or
                    not
                        she's
                                  loved.

                Make a Wish, Darling

Diagnosis

The drought came
with the volcano.

Street lamps
frowned through
ash-made dark.

Homes turned
into hills with
chimneys peeking
out the summits.

We hummed
as we trudged
through the wreckage,
until our hums
turned into songs.

We didn't know
what else to do.

Tears wouldn't
water the grass.

Cries wouldn't call
the birds home.

I am the pale girl statue,
arms raised, afraid of the ocean
                overcoming her lungs
                          with salt.

I am the driftwood boat
filled with flowers and bones
                awaiting the arrow flame
                        to sink me.

Waves Away

Four Quatrains and a Line in Acceptance of Begrudged Hope

& we all know our pulses will stop
stretching out our skin, someday
we'll no longer inhale guilt, exhale regret,
we'll sleep without steeping our sheets.

Won't we let these trite affirmations
of stone peek out from the river
eddies, let them show us how
to overcome the current?

Yes, we invite the hooks to lodge
between our shoulder blades,
hold our skeletons at attention,
invite another under our chins.

Here we are biting back the bitterness
toward the unknowing stranger who greets
us with a sing-song good morning
in the slush, sleet seeping in our socks.

We welcome the cardinal who appears
on the fence or mailbox or telephone wire,
its relentless call, waiting for us to answer,
for us to say good morning to you, too,

waiting for us to say anything, to do anything at all.

October

I haven't even written it yet,
but I'm already annoyed
by what I'm going to write.

Cling to gratitude.

I am an empty box, flattened and discarded. Boiling
tomato sauce, staining the countertop and floor. A wayward cinder
that found its way to a Californian forest in the middle of July.

I hate that
My Dad Has Terminal Cancer
is my new
normal.

A little less than a month has sprinted by since
I found out my father had a year
to check off whatever boxes remained on his to-do list.

Eleven months and three days left.

This is now my life,
this is now *his* life,

                    his death.

In the last less-than-a-month, I have cried
until my irises scraped like sandpaper against my lids,
I have screamed like a hammer
on piano keys. I have collapsed
in the shower, let my body lay splayed
in self-pity and in grief.
I have fallen asleep
crying,
I have woken up

crying.
I have gone to work
in my pajamas—
                    but at least I went to work.
I have cried
in individual therapy.
I have cried
in group therapy.
                Yes, I go to both,
and I hope I'm better for it, but I suspect
I am still a nightmare,
                        just with less money.

I am a ghost town,
my body still exists among the remnants and relics,
but no one lives here anymore.
The locals moved out
with the post office. The shelves
at the corner store stand as tombstones
marking the prices of items
that once waited for hands
to toss them in their basket.
Spiders and the remains of their kills fill
the fluorescent lights.
The crows don't even stop on the wires
when they fly over.
I am a ghost town,

but I have also smiled.
I have also laughed.
I have also blushed
when a handsome man put his hand in my hair.

I watched my friend sing Bobby McGee
better than Janis Joplin ever could.

I took a swing dance lesson. I admired
art and went to the movies. I curled
my hair and put on makeup for a fancy dinner date,
I kissed a stunning man in the snowy street.

   And,
       it's all been done with a plastic bag over
       my head
       duct taped at the neck.

When my dad found out
        The News

he said

I'm happy.
I've had a great life.
I've been married to my best friend
for forty-two years
      with no drama!
My kids never got into any (big) trouble.
I've traveled.
I've done good work.
I've helped my communities.
And I'm not sad
or angry.

Then he said,

I'm happy.

He's happy.
He's happy.

         I am not happy.
       I am a cut-out paper doll
        version of myself
        covered in maggots.

Yet, I have found that through the maggots,
I am still capable of joyful moments, I can still
find glimmers of gratitude that make me feel less dead,
less like I'm rotting from the inside out and a little more
blessed. I need to cling to these glimmers of gratitude
to stay afloat, to not submerge further into the murk.

My sadness is a thousand-foot well,

g
r
a
t
i
t
u
d
e

is

a

r
o
p
e

keeping me from drowning.

Glimmer of Gratitude #1: I love my dad.

My close friend, Lauren, lost her dad to cancer,
pancreatic cancer, in July of 2014. He was given a year
and lived for six,

four of which Lauren described as
really good.

She and my other friends, loose acquaintances, and strangers
who have experienced the brutal hollowing of loss
have laid out a map for me. They have been through this journey
already, and they are the ones whom I can trust
to authentically help me in my own journey into the dank cave.
They are the only ones who can describe the skulls
lining the catacombs, the only ones who can waft
the stench of loneliness, who can echo the rasp of futility.

She said,

So it doesn't last forever,
our lives together on Earth.
That's okay.
It's meaningful, and I'd rather have this grief
than a dad I don't talk to or hate...
We both know people that have horrid parents.
It's an honor to love someone so much
that their sickness is eviscerating to think about.

I never thought I would feel lucky
to have pain dripping from my pores,
pain stuck to the pads of my fingers,
to the bottoms of my feet, to have pain become
the core of my identity in an instant,

but here I am.

I'm walking my parents' beagle, Molly, when a stranger
in his driveway sees me. He knows
I had to be Anne Marie even before I introduce myself.
He heard I'd be coming from Wyoming
to spend this time with my parents. And this man,
who I learned later was one of their close friends, said:

Is that Molly?

It is. I'm Terry and Kathy's daughter.

For a moment the moment
is so normal. Until…

I'm really sorry to hear about your dad.
He's one heck of a nice guy.

As if I'm hearing

The News

for the first time again.
Burning chest.
Seashell ears.

Molly sniffs at the man's hands, always checking
to see if anyone has a biscuit hidden in their fist.
        Sometimes they do.

The man becomes a blur. If he says anything else,
I can't hear him over my own refrain.
Sobbing has become my chorus now,
a wretched tune wrenched between each verse.

I don't know his name, I don't know
how he knows my dad,
but he puts his arm around me.

Thank you for saying that.
He is. He is one heck of a nice guy.

One heck of a nice guy.
I know my reputation does not compare to that,
but I aspire to be better
so that one day, upon hearing my name,
someone might say,
She's one heck of a nice person.

I am grateful my dad is one heck of a nice guy,
that I am a twenty-story building
who had its first floor supports laced
with explosives by his cancer diagnosis,
that I am just waiting
to be detonated.

It is better
than feeling

nothing.

Glimmer of Gratitude #2: I have somewhat of a warning

When my mother told me
                    The News
it felt like my wrists
had been slashed and every drop of my blood
spilled out of me. Bones and cartilage, too,
every nerve and synapse.
I am only a pile of fat and tissue—

                    Existing,
                but no longer
                    alive.

Every heartbreak,
every disappointment,
every romance
who didn't love me,
every friend
who stabbed me in the back
                    or in the front,
every job
that passed me over,
every precious belonging

I lost or broke,
every financial downturn
are just dead leaves
along the trail
that crunch under my feet.

I will at least be able to say goodbye.

I will be able to say what I need to say and do what I need to do.

I will be able to cherish every moment as if it's our last
                                because it will be.

I have the opportunity for closure and peace
when so many people are not granted that same blessing.
Ruptured aneurysms, heart attacks, overdoses, suicides, car accidents
all pluck loved ones from this world without warning like a child
grabbing at dandelions in a yard, ripping away
the petals, chanting *He loves me, He loves me not,* yellow dying
tiny fingers like blood stains. These thefts don't allow
for the same interim period leading up to death, which conjures
up its own lineup of blessings and curses. I am grateful for

the doom.

I'd rather share my time with the dread
than have no time at all.

Glimmer of Gratitude #3: I am (somewhat of) an adult.

My childhood was not cannonballed
by my dad's illness. I only had to love my childhood dog,
not even feed her or walk her. I earned mostly A's
in school, crying if I received a B+. No relatives
abused me. Physically or otherwise. My sister and I
never gave each other stitches. We each were student diplomats
and exchange students. She played tennis. I was a cheerleader.

My childhood and my young adulthood were not interrupted
by the shocking and disorienting news
that I would soon lose a parent or, worse,
I had already lost them without any warning.

My friend, Daphne, lost her mother to cancer,
her sole caregiver, when she was only single-digits-old.
Her father wasn't in her life,
So when her mother lost her fight
against her own body, she went
to live with her grandmother.
But then Daphne's grandmother passed away, too.

It's a miracle to me that Daphne could withstand the anguish
of back to back deaths and still grow up
into an emotionally adept adult,
polyglot, world traveler, published author, pedagogical guru.
And now mother to her own daughter.
All without bitterness swirling in her morning coffee,
without acrid contempt living in her belly
like it does in mine.

I think about my friend, Dave, who was just a little fuck-up
of a kid, twenty-one, when he lost his dad to cancer.
He had to become
his dad's sole caregiver,
after his dad had been his sole caregiver.
Dave worked part-time in the day as a teacher's aid
and part-time at night as a custodian for a law firm.
He was working and working out
his place in this world.

I remember him sending me a photo of himself
while cleaning the law office. He wore dress pants
and a long-sleeved, button-up, white collar shirt.

Dress for the job you want,
　　　　　　　　　　he said

Having to enter adulthood, navigate utility bills,
car insurance, and taxes at the same time as caring
for my parent at the end of their life
is too much for me to comprehend.

If that stress wasn't enough, while Dave's dad was slowly dying
at home, his emotional support, his long-term girlfriend,
was finding romance in someone else's bed.

He told me he knew about it the whole time, but—
and I totally get this—having his girlfriend with him,
even though duplicitous and deceitful, was better
than being alone.

I imagine my ribcage like a rusted-out wheel well
of a 1989 Pontiac, but I live in my own place,
I pay my own bills. I don't rely on my parents
for money, and they don't rely on me for money.
We only rely on each other
for presence.

Glimmer of Gratitude #4: I am not alone.

When I first found out
　　　　　　　　The News

my mind went to who I didn't have in my life. My loneliness
acted as stakes, pinning my grief shroud on top of me.

I risked feeling even more alone
by asking Bert to come be with me.
But Bert said *yes*.

　　　　　I wonder who I might have settled for, if I didn't have him,

just to have warm skin against mine, just to smell
someone's breath while I fell asleep.

He and I met in the spring. He thought I was great,
but his enthusiasm scared me like a squirrel trapped
in a backyard shed staring at the child in the door
who only wishes to stroke its fur.

He brings me flowers too often.

I pushed him away. He tried to convince me
not to leave. I left anyway.

Most people are not like my shitty ex, AJ, but I still
felt relieved when Bert didn't call me names or tell me
I was going to die alone. He didn't tell me
how stupid I was for walking away
from something so good. He just let me be.

When he reached out occasionally to be friends,
I declined his invitations, imagining only
the shackle he could have hiding behind his back.

When I started dating someone else, Bert still asked
to spend time together. My acquiescence, then, became
a kind of friendship
contract we both signed.
I double checked for hidden small print,
for lawyering tricks.
Bert couldn't expect more,
and if he did,
that would be on him,
not me.

We met for lunch and talked about the terrible people
from Tinder we had gone on dates with and how the new idiot
I was dragging around

was still married.

Bert attended an event I organized for my work.
He fixed my dog gate.
He helped me plan
renovations to my office.
He high-fived me
when I dumped the married idiot.
He held me
as I sobbed over my dad having cancer.

I had a moment of reckoning:
Bert lost his title of "stranger."
He witnessed me eat an entire sleeve of saltine crackers
that I used as spoons for a tub of butter, watched me
use my sleeve as a tissue as snot dripped down my lips
then kissed those lips when I asked him to.

We had emotional intimacy whether I wanted it or not.

It was an accident,
but no takesies backsies.

When emotional intimacy turned out not to be
the pit of fang-exposed taipans I imagined it being,
I decided I liked it after all.

> Maybe I only like it with him.

> It doesn't hurt that he's got bear eyes to match his bear hugs.

I could have ended up completely alone and isolated,
but I didn't.

> I have my mom.
> I have my sister.
> I have my dad
> still.

I have a plethora of acquaintances
who stepped up to help me when they had no reason to.
I have an abundance of friends
who have thatched together their arms
just to carry me above the mud.

I have Bert.
Really have him.
We decide to get married.
No time like the present.

                              I'll be able to have
                         the moment of walking
                                down the aisle
                               hand-in-hand
                               with my father
                                   after all.

I am grateful *to myself*
for pulling my head out of my ass,
for being open enough
to receive Bert's kindness and love.

                                      Finally.

_____

                     Step 1: Fuck off.
                 Step 2: Accept help.
                  Step 3: Gratitude.

I Now Know

as admirers stare at Hibiscus wondering
how the gods created a tongue and mouth

delicate enough to steep and swallow, she wills
rough hands to pluck her from her stem to end

her ignored screams. They don't see how
she trumpets her despair to the insects. They

do not hear her over their own buzz. They don't
want to know her as anything other than pretty.

A body thrashes
when it only needs to stand
in the shallowness.

Elegy
A ribcage
After Athena Liu

Mourning songs prod my dammed chest up the mountainside
[like]
Sisyphus who cheated death too many times for
[the]
gods to accept it. Air slithers into my lungs,
[furled]
up on themselves; they search for a resurrection
[fern]
to show them the meaning of renewal. I climb
[on]
aware of the maddening non-ending that is
[an]
antediluvian hope there'd be more than just
[oak]
urns after summiting, lifeless stone at my feet.
[I'm]
awake at 3 AM, asleep at noon, eyes sink,
[drained]
like hourglass sand. I hum myself a prelude
[but]
my soles only slug their way uphill, and I can
[not]
stop wondering what it truly means to raise the
[dead.]

My Father Says

he's not sure, he'll have to check
his stash for my mother's breakfast
cereal. She chuckles under her breath,
swatting her hand in the air as if
telling her high school sweetheart
he's being naughty. In the waiting
room of the oncology ward, my father
tells my mother to choose a magazine
that won't hurt her if she falls asleep,
and her laugh leaves her mouth like
a fire engine, echoing through the high
ceilings, makes other withered patients
turn to stare with angry eyebrows.
My mother grabs her purse from the side
table, tosses it over her shoulder on her way
out the door to visit a neighbor, and my father
asks if she's planning another domino heist.
I don't know what they're talking about.
I am not privy to their flirtations, to their
inside jokes. I only watch the scenes in study,
analyzing every interaction, observing what
it looks like to share a life with your best friend,
learning how it's done.

My enemy will someday hold their dying love
in their arms, and their crooked hole of a mouth,

screaming, anguished, into the air, will create
my next breath. We will share the same chorus

of pain, the unspoken song that unites us,
the universal refrain that asks us to bless

this world for its suffering;
the only thing that builds

The Bridge to Empathy

Sepsis

I listened to my father pray
for the first responders
to arrive, his words sought
his Father to

Please, Lord, let them get here
soon, Lord, please.

             I remembered waking
             from a nightmare
             in my childhood home,
             my words searched
             for my father to

             Dad, please, come get me,
             please. Dad.

             He relieved my panic
             walking through my bedroom door.
             I wished to be grown to know
             what it felt like
             to fear nothing.

My father, at seventy-four, pleads
for his Father to come get him
and wishes to know what it feels like
to not have pain.
And he has no fear,
just as I imagined.

January

We all want to collar control
in uncontrollable situations,
leash a chain to its neck,
wrap the links in a wrist-locked grip.

My family and I cannot control
that my father is dying. We cannot control
his lung cancer. We don't like it, we don't want it,
but there's no way to un-die his body, there's no way
to un-cancer his lungs. If only love
could keep him alive, he would live
forever.

My mom obsesses over the guest
bathroom. The sink must remain empty, bare of any hints
of use. No toiletries may be visible, not even
my electric toothbrush. Nothing can be left
in the bathroom garbage.
No tissues, no paper towels.
No signs of life.

As nonsensical as I find it to be, I agree to it.
I don't want to fight. When lung cancer
is the feral cat evading a catch pole,
the guest bathroom became the gerbil
my mother could ostracize to its terrarium.

She can't cure my dad's cancer, but
she can make sure the guest bathroom is spotless.

My aunt is a Catholic Eucharistic minister.
She brings communion to my dad every day.

                                        Every.
                                        Day.

It makes her feel better.
It probably makes my mom feel better.
Maybe it makes my dad feel better,
though I suspect he participates because
it makes my mom feel better,
and he cares about my mom
more than anything else.

My sister takes time off work every month
to be in Florida with us.
She and my mother work morning through night
to pack up a life's worth of belongings and memories:
evenings watching Jeopardy and drinking wine,
game nights and inside jokes move
to their new one-bedroom among the many
identical units within their independent living facility.
Years of piano lessons, world-traveling visitors,
and ancestors' lives find their way into a storage locker.
Christmas ornaments, knickknacks, and garden décor
find new homes through Goodwill. Losing
lottery tickets, kindergarten finger paintings,
and unfinished crafts die in Tuesday morning's trash pickup.

My sister can't cure our dad's cancer,
but she can sort seven decades of a life,
set the destinies of its contents into motion.

Bert takes time off work too
to stand next to me,
sit next to me,
lay next to me.
Next to a dry-rotted log.

Even though I'm joyless.
Sexless.
Loveless.

Even though things
in many ways
have been

                             less

between us.

He repairs the broken tiles on the counter
in my parents' old house, the house they retired to,
the house they were going to live in until they died.
Here they are, living out their plan.

Bert paints their front door
and everyone who visits asks
if they bought a new one.
He patches the holes in the walls
where their art used to hang,
rehangs their art on the walls
in their new apartment.

He spoons me at night and listens to me cry.
Doesn't tell me it's going to be okay.
Doesn't tell me how things could be worse.

I can't yell at my dad's cancer,
so I yell at Bert.

Sometimes he yells back.
Mostly he doesn't.

He is my gerbil to contain,
to handle when I feel like
then put back in his tank.

I don't know what we're doing
but I suspect we wouldn't be getting married
if my dad weren't dying.

I wonder if he's only marrying me
still
because my dad is dying.
I suspect he is.

Makes me love him more.

I wonder if we both have the same thought
of going through the motions,
of giving everyone something to look forward to
instead of fear.
We'll quit the masquerade
once it's

over.
I don't ask him.
Worry cowers my tongue behind my teeth.
I want my father to see me in my mother's wedding dress,
to die knowing I did it,
that I won't spend the rest of my life
keeping anyone who wants to love me
an arm's length away.
Even if it's a lie.

Bert can't cure my dad's cancer,
but he can be helpful, make sure
my mom doesn't have to hire out household services.
He can't cure my dad's cancer,
but he can smile in front of my parents,
sit next to me on the couch, holding my hand,
my head on his shoulder even after
I spent the day not making eye contact
with him because he wouldn't
tell the Starbucks barista he asked for an americano
instead of the macchiato he received
and wouldn't drink it because it was too sweet
and wouldn't let me tell them either.
It doesn't matter

when my father is dying.
Anger drips from my brow,
and I only have Robert
to pat it dry.

Perhaps he is my guest bathroom, my daily communion,
my piles labeled for storage, donation, or trash.

We're never aware of our own nonsense.

I control my presence in my dad's presence,
resign from my job, even though
they made allowances for me to work remotely,
then half time,
then quarter time.

It's hard to give a shit about budgets and board meetings,
payroll deadlines, and grant applications
when your idol's eyelashes flutter away in clumps.
All those unwished wishes wasted.

I try to control my dad's skin,
destroyed by the chemo,
particularly on his hands and feet.
Every night for months,
I rub his feet with Aquaphor,
his back, face, and hands with lotion.
I don't know if it does anything
or if he enjoys it
or if he knows that I just need something to control.

His cancer stole the feeling
from his palms and his fingertips.
He can't hold utensils, so I hold them for him.
He can't hold pills, so I feed them to him.
His new life of constant sitting has worn

away the skin behind his thighs, even the little
of him that remains is too heavy
for comfort.

I buy him the most expensive cushions
for his wheelchair and recliner.
He yells at me about the cost.
I tell him it cost nothing,
that they fell off the back of a truck.

I am here,
in Florida.
Left my mountain life behind
as if everything I built for myself there meant nothing,
because it did
in comparison to my father's life,
the wealth of time I had squandered for so long,
never thinking one day the coffers would run dry.

I can't cure my dad's cancer,
but I can make sure his skin is moisturized. I can
make sure he gets his medicine. I can
make sure he has the best cushion. I can
make sure that he is never alone when my mom is busy
          deciding whether
          her belongings are meaningful enough
          to keep or if they should be thrown away.

My sister and I can't cure our dad's cancer.
We couldn't control that he was too sick
to go to the restaurant where my mom had a reservation
for her 70th birthday.
But we could order lobster tail dinner take-out
and a birthday cake for the last birthday
my dad would share with my mom
or with any of our family members.

We can't cure our dad's cancer,
but we can be here.

My dad's oncologist recommends
he no longer pursue treatment.

She can see his withered body
and spirit.

We all can.

My mom can't control my dad's cancer,
but she can schedule an appointment
with his pulmonologist for a second
opinion, like a child asking their other parent
for permission to go out on a school night.

The pulmonologist says my dad can
continue treatment. So we go—
my father, mother, and I—
for a follow-up with his oncologist, who plans
a new regimen: instead of three chemo drugs,
only one will course through his cells
raze every village in its wake—
no hostages, only casualties.
Whether one militia poisons the water or three,
the fish still all die.

My dad asks,

> *What is it going to do for me?*

The oncologist explains to him, to us, how the drug works,
details the physiological responses.
She and my mom discuss what the second cycle of chemo

will look like after that, and I watch my father stare
at the ground, the slightest shake of his head.

Like a sycamore leaf in November,
stem whimpering as it held onto its branch
with a weakening grip, I witnessed
the moment my father was ready
to let go.

His vocal cords are as paralyzed
as the rest of his body. He can't speak
any louder than a whisper. I can see him try
to interrupt, see fatigue over take his attempt.
He has been sitting upright for over an hour—
a long time for him—the exhaustion shows
in his shoulders hunched
like a sunflower under an overcast sky.

I interrupt for him, say
what I know he wants to say.

Dad, is this what you want to do?

Mom and the oncologist stop talking.

Or would you rather not?

He looks at my mom with welling eyes, says,

I'd rather not.

She cries into her hands.

He says,

I'm sorry, Dear. I'm sorry,

as if he is letting her down.
She's spent four months
of the bout rubbing his shoulders
in the corner of the ring, encouraging
him, *Anything is possible. Anything.*

But it's not her body he has to peel
off the ground after each blow,
not her cauliflower ears,
not her bruised kidneys.
It's not her blood he spits out.

I cannot cure his cancer,
but I can rise from my chair,
put my arms around both of them,
rub my forehead into his arm.
I can say,
                    You don't need to be sorry for being lovable.

Which he is. Loved by everyone.

Tears fill the oncologist's eyes too.
I see the clench in her jaw, watch her
swallow the bitterness of her profession.
Not everyone can be saved.

She agrees:
continuing treatment
will make his life
worse.

She can't cure his cancer,
but she can be honest.

I can imagine her going home that night,
crying into the arms of the person

with the wedding band that matches hers.
> *I couldn't save a patient today.*
> *And he's one hell of a nice guy.*

My dad can't cure his own cancer,
but he can control how he spends
the life he has left.

The oncologist refers him to hospice.
She can't cure his cancer,
but she can control whether he's comfortable.

Now, everybody's goal is to control whether he's comfortable.

The oncologist says,
> *I'm going to prescribe that you do something*
> *you love every day.*

Today, we watch the Australian Open.
Dad loves tennis.

And we wait.

We can't control my dad's cancer.
We can't cure it.
But we can watch the ESPN with him.
We can make sure one of us is in his room
every minute of every day.

I sleep in the chair in the corner of his room
each night, not sleeping. Leave in the morning
when my mother arrives so I can feed and walk
my dog. Feed and walk myself. Sleep
in my parents' bed for an hour. Cry
in my parents' shower for an hour.

I can't control my dad's cancer.
But I can control my hatred, resentment, and bitterness,
vindictiveness, contempt, and despair.
These emotions take me away
from my dad, transport me
to the past and the future,

where he does not live.

So I control them.

At least in front of him.

Step 1: Fuck off.
Step 2: Accept help.
Step 3: Gratitude.
Step 4: Maintain control.

Holding the shell of the man he used to be to my ear,
his tidal voice crashed ashore, calling me
to watch a nest of turtles

break free from their sandy womb, frantic to find
their ocean mother; a race from first breath
to moonlit waves.

I Will Remember You This Way, I Promise
After Andrea Gibson

Stone-Faced

on this stone sink
his full moon head stared
as empty as my stolen breath.
He learned anew how to worship
like a boy among candles
and wreathed flowers,
the way Mary prayed
below six crossed feet,
her two lungs anchors
in a porcelain basin.

Remembering December

I can't remember what I said
to my father in his wheelchair

after he returned from Humiston Beach for what
we knew would be the last time. I remember

how he described the sunset with his eyes closed,
clinging to the fire colors waltzing across the ocean

surface in his memory, how he quaked his hand,
recreating the refracted beams dancing onto the caverns

of his face. But I can't remember what I said

in response, if I expressed how glad I was
he had a final visit, if I acknowledged how

important the moment was as death sprinted
for his etiolated body. I hope I said the right

words. But I can't be sure. I've let others down
more than once, and I've let myself down

more times than that.

I scream at the ocean
Why, why, why?
And with every wave
breaking on sand, She replies,
Shh, shh, shh.

February

I stand at the lectern of the church, looking out
at all of my father's friends,
at my sister, my mother,
my aunt, my Bert.
      I wear a white dress
I bought in October
from Goodwill for $6 because
when I paraded through the living room
displaying my thrift shop finds, my father said,

     Wow, great dress!

White with crimson and navy flowers,
cinched at the waist. Short sleeves.

I will not wear my mother's wedding gown. Will not walk,
hand in hand with my father, down the aisle.

Instead, I walk hand in hand with Bert
down the aisle behind my father's casket.

I begin.

    Thank you, everyone, for coming here today to celebrate my father.

                   I had the honor of caring for my dad
             in his illness, had the honor of holding his hand
                       as he transitioned from
                          relative to ancestor.

                    This evening, I have the honor
                       of telling you all
                    about his incredible life.

My father was born in a small factory town
in upstate New York. There, he and his brother
had a standard American upbringing filled

with paper routes, Little League, and Boy Scouts.
He was proud, even late in life, of achieving
the rank of Eagle Scout.

He attended college in Oswego.
Though he majored in Physics, his stories
about college almost always revolved
around his time working with his friends
at a horse stable on campus.

For years after he graduated, he drove for two hours
each way on most weekends to continue working there—
not because it paid well, but because he loved it.

In 1970, he started working at GE and developed
his career over time to become a computer programmer,
a position he retained for nearly four decades before he retired.

In 1976, he met his soulmate, the love of his life,
his best friend, and my mother
on a blind date at a bowling alley.
He had a bit of work to do to impress her,
but his natural charm, wit, and gentle demeanor
won her over.

Their love and marriage has served
as a quintessential example of what true love is
for their children and for everyone
who interacts with them.

My father was a great man.

Not because he was a millionaire
or had a fancy job. He didn't drive
a luxury car or wear the best clothing.
He did not hold rank, title, or office.
He did not start a movement.

He was a great man simply

because he was kind.

When I first came to Florida to be with my dad,
while walking my parents' beloved beagle,
a gentleman stopped me because he recognized the dog.

I'm so sorry to hear about your dad.
He's one heck of a nice guy.

It's hard to behold the acrid taste of loss
as a blessing, to recognize

pain only comes from the grief of losing someone
who has had such a profound and loving impact
on your life. My dad was one heck of a nice guy.

I ask everyone here to ask themselves:
Is that what people would say about you?
If it's not, let me give you a few ideas
of how you can earn that title
based on the many wonderful things my father did
for others.

First, participate in every food drive.
Not just with a can of tuna,
but with a case of tuna. An entire box

of non-perishable goods.
Be the reason why the food drive is successful.

Be the reason the blood bank stays open.
Donate blood and donate platelets
We often saw my dad with a bandage around each arm
because he donated as often as is legally allowed.

Do all of the chores for forty years
and never complain.
Laundry, grocery shopping, dishes,
mowing the lawn, gardening,
walking the dog, cleaning the litter box,
shoveling snow, fixing the car…

Become a recycling champion,
and not just in your own home.
Walk around your neighborhood
picking up the litter you see.
Go to sports fields after games
and pick recyclables out of garbage cans.

When you visit a cemetery,
bring extra flowers and leave them at a grave
that has no caretaker. Pull weeds away
from the stones that are overgrown. Brush
the dirt from the embossed letters that you pass.
Bring your own lawnmower to tame
the grass pathways, and eventually,
buy a riding lawnmower
with your own money, become
the unofficial groundskeeper
all without compensation or recognition.

When you pick someone up
from the airport, bring their favorite snacks

and leave them on the passenger seat for them. Don't tell.
Just let them find the goodies and enjoy the surprise.

Keep a list of your friends' birthdays so you never forget
to send a card. And when you send a card,
cover it with stickers.

Walk on the beach—Humiston beach was his favorite.
Say hello to everyone you pass—and, of course,
pick up any trash you see along the way.

When your neighbor's outdoor light is out,
change the bulb for them.
When your neighbor down the street's outdoor light is out,
change the bulb for them too.
Then, start carrying light bulbs in your pockets
when you walk at night just in case.

If you dislike someone, simply say, "they're okay."
It's not weak or false because
they more than likely are okay... in some way.

When you're walking your dog
and you see a dog mess
that was not from your dog,
pick it up anyway.

Invite strangers into your home
from all over the world.
Not just for a meal, but for months.
Be their headquarters,
a place they can return to for years to come.

When a song reminds you of your partner,
reach for their hand,
tell them, This song is us.
Hold their hand while you listen

to it together, feeling the love between you.

Tell your loved ones you love them every day.
Every. Day.
Sign off your emails, end your phone calls with
Love Ya.

When you hug someone,
give them a little shake.

Be silly, even when you're in a hospital
gown finding out what true indignity is.
Be silly. Make jokes.
Have the humility of the Dalai Lama or Pope Francis.

These are just a few of the many, many examples
of my dad's kindness and good nature
with which we were blessed. I have hundreds more;
I'm sure everyone here does.
We would love to hear them.

No matter how I showed kindness
toward my dad, no matter how many days,
weeks, months I helped care for him,
it does not feel like I can begin to thank him
for everything he did for me
during my thirty-three years.

No one can compare to him in selflessness.

My dad was one heck of a nice person,
and I pray that we all continue
his legacy of kindness. Imagine
the domino effect we might have on the world
if we did.

One person, my dad, had an impact
on every one of us sitting here today.
Imagine what we could do collectively
for the world if we all performed
an act of kindness every day.

Thank you, Dad.
Thank you, thank you, thank you,
for setting a good example.

Step 1: Fuck off.
Step 2: Accept help.
Step 3: Gratitude.
Step 4: Maintain control.
Step 5: Remember.

Eta Ursae Majoris

away

inch
an
of
ths
sand
thou
four
&
years
light
sand
thou
from four
watches
the sky he
when I search
his light
its light
while embodying
the path of alkaid
now he follows
who created them
older than the deities
older than the hunters' myths
present as he became
he lost
into the breath
relative to ancestor
transition from
i felt him

11:20 PM

My mother's voice bit my undead face like an electric eel. Her cries begged for answers, begged for air through the shock like she woke to an assassin holding a pillow to her nose and mouth. I ran barefoot to my car, my phone to my ear. Where were my shoes? I had to get her, had to bring her to her husband. Dead. *Are you sure, Honey? Are you sure? Did a nurse tell you?* And it took all the marrow in my jaws to respond, *A nurse didn't have to tell me, Mom. A nurse didn't have to tell me.* I could hear my parents' beagle whimpering—my mother's beagle. *Why didn't you call me?* she screamed over and over, choking between each why. *There wasn't time, Mom,* I pleaded. *There wasn't time. There wasn't time. There wasn't time. There wasn't time. There wasn't time.*

I think of the last
shadows his body cast, how
crematories work.

Gravestone Flowers

I paced my father's hometown cemetery
as he pushed and pulled his lawn mower

through the overgrown grass, planted marigolds
at strangers' graves. I ripped dandelions

with the ferocity of a child who was Anne
with an E and who pretended to be the one

from Green Gables, who didn't care to understand
what it meant to be dead. I held the bouquet

like a bride and trampled the wild blades, wondering
why my dad cared at all to tend the plots of those

decaying for a century. Now, with a longer life
of collected memories, I know he'd always been

the man to shovel his neighbor's driveway
in December, to walk at night with lightbulbs

in his pockets to replace anyone's burned out
porch lamps while they slept, and he couldn't

let his parents' bones lie in a graveyard replete with
Jumanji canopies taking over the signs that someone

once inhaled this town, that someone once exhaled
this town. Now I adorn my father's grave with seashells,

arrange them in a circle around a ceramic frog. I carry
his funeral flowers like a baby in my arms, lay one at

a time across barren graves near his. And maybe
visiting strangers will be touched to see a lily, even

desiccated from the sun, atop their loved one's grave.
Maybe this was my father's sentiment too. Maybe he

thought not of those who passed on, but of those
who would pass by; they would know someone

cared enough. Or maybe they would think
it was their ancestors' way of saying hi

from the other side. And maybe,
when you think about it, it was.

Remains of a Man

I wonder if your refrigerated flesh burned as I cried
in the shower, if I reached for the tub edge, dizzy
as flames engulfed your knees and hips and feet, if
that's when I watched shampoo swill the drain,
clogged by my hair and spit.

I wonder if a chimney coughed you out somewhere, if
the sky choked on your ash one last time. I wonder
if I missed your papal farewell not knowing
where to look, or if I saw your body
that night, a smoke ring around the moon.

My Father Is

the heart-shaped cloud at Humiston beach
on valentine's day / the meteor like jade on fire
breaching the stratosphere that one night /
        he is *on the road again* on the radio
as fireworks celebrate the new year / one year
greater than the one etched into his grave / he is
the big dipper faint / in the orange sky visible
for only a moment before the fluorescence of the street
lamps steals him away / he is my mother's instinctive
go ask your father / he is the tenth of a second I don't
remember that I can't / he is my right eye hooded more
than my left / my voice at the cemetery scolding my fragility
     as I lie in the gravel a sobbing heap
                    of contortions / *we all die we all die we all die* /
     he is my hand in my hair / my breath
my throat consoling
       it's okay it's okay it's okay

When Cardinals Appear

Bandit bird, thief within the cherry blossoms
stealing worries and ruminations, replacing

the *what ifs* with the down-slurred whistles
of a long song, a soul song, a sailing song,

connecting me on this earthly plane
like an isthmus to my ancestors, flitting

from your perch between branches as if it means nothing
at all to share my father's message from the other side.

It is just another day, just another message.

Twelve Days Later

When I first began writing
about this journey, I attempted to navigate
my thoughts and emotions by searching for the steps
as if a How-To Guide to tragedy existed.

With no experience to reference,
I've been living
the guide the last five months,
figuring out these five steps.

> Step 1: Fuck off.
> Step 2: Accept help.
> Step 3: Gratitude.
> Step 4: Maintain control.
> Step 5: Remember.

Now, I have come to Step 6:

> Chaotically repeat.

My father passed away.

On his last day on this Earth,
he had a really good day—as good a day
as a person can have while bedridden,
experiencing the role reversal of parent and child.
Thirty-three years after bathing me,
diapering me, and spoon feeding me,
he accepted it was his turn to be cared for.

I watched my father care for my grandparents
at the end of their lives,
watched my father lead his mother,
brain obliterated by dementia,
into the upstairs bathroom for a shower,

put her pajamas on her frail frame,
and help her into her bed.

I wonder if he watched his mother
do the same for her parents.
If he had the same example set for him
that he set for me.

The nurses in hospice could care for him with kindness,
but they could not care for him with love.
Only I could do that,

and I was honored to provide him that care.

He deserved it.

As my dad rested in his hospice bed listening to music,
Juice Newton's "Sweetest Thing" came on.

I was writing the poems in this collection
when movement in my periphery caught
my attention. My dad, his eyes still closed, reached
his hand out for my mom seated next to him knitting.

She grabbed his hand, and he whispered,
                              This song is us.

They both let the tears fall without words.
I cried, holding back any sound
so as not to interrupt their moment. At the end
of the song, my mother stood up
and laid her chest across his.

She said,
          You know I love you, Honey. So much.

My dad whispered back,
  Me too. Me too.

In the afternoon, I gave him a sponge bath, rubbed lotion
into his skin. I shaved his face and told him
his eyelashes were starting to grow back.
I trimmed his nails and massaged Aquaphor into his feet
and legs. We, as a family, were always telling each other
we loved each other in acts of service and quality time
rather than words alone.

He had banana cream pie for dinner.

We watched TV, somehow finding
moments of laughter together.
Not knowing it would be the last time he'd laugh.

A little after 11 PM, I held his hand
as he took his final breaths.

I told him he was safe.
I told him he was fine.

I hate that I said those things.
Those stupid things.

Of course he wasn't fine.
I wasn't thinking.

Of course I wasn't thinking.

I also told him I loved him,
that I wasn't leaving him. I told him
he wasn't alone, that he was such a good dad. I hope
I said those things more. I hope
I said them and didn't shout them

as all I wanted to do was scream.
Scream,

No! Dad! Don't leave me!

But I can't remember.

I fainted.

Woke up on the chair on the other side of the room, my chair.
The nurse caught me when I fell,
and he carried me in his arms to that place I slept
every night for two weeks.

I staggered out of my father's room
and out of the building in my stocking feet
still dizzy with shock.
Maybe I imagined it.
Maybe I imagined the whole thing.
Maybe I am drunk or high.
Maybe I am escaping a hospital where I am the patient.

The nurses yelled after me as I left, told me
I should sit for a little bit longer. But I couldn't.
I had to get to my mother.

She answered the phone
with the sing-songy *Hello*
customary to our family.
The same hello my sister uses
to answer the phone.
The one I used to use.
I told my mother

The News

and her scream shattered the entire world.
I imagine on the other side of the ocean, a child

stopped in the middle of their game of hopscotch
because they could hear my mother's
ventricles, and atria, and valves
all rendering apart.

Are you sure, Honey? Are you sure?
Did a nurse tell you? Did a nurse say so?

> All I could say was,
> *A nurse didn't have to tell me, Mom.*
> *A nurse didn't have to tell me.*

Why didn't you call me?
I would've come over to be with him!

> *There wasn't time, Mom.*
> *You wouldn't have made it.*
> *I couldn't leave dad,*
> *not even for a second to call you.*
> *There wasn't time.*

> And there wasn't.
> Really, there wasn't.

And now, I feel like I've returned to the beginning
of all of this. I've returned to September 13th.
I'm sure I answered the phone with a sing-songy *Hello*
before my mother told my father was going to die.
The burning chest, the seashell ears.
The same wondering:

> *What do I do? What are the steps?*

Even though I knew my father was going to die,
even though it was said and unsaid over and over again,
even though we knew it was his last Thanksgiving, his last

Christmas, his last New Year on this planet, it still seemed
impossible.

I believed I was going to live in that hospice room with him
For much longer than I did. And I would have.
I would have lived there,
eaten meals off of plastic trays,
slept neck cocked in the chair,
ears alert to any sound my father made.
Forever.

Two great pains mark my grief trail like cairns:
knowing that it was going to happen,
and it happening.
But unlike cairns, I can never navigate
back the way I came.
These two towers of rocks
Come with the same guide,
though, I believe.

Step 1: Fuck off.

I unfriended over 200 people
from the modest 400 friends I used to have
on social media.

I need this space for catharsis,
to expel all of the hatred, resentment,
and bitterness, vindictiveness,
contempt, and despair
I've harbored.

Dozens of people,
not just friends, but some people I barely know
sent me messages of condolence. People I haven't spoken to
in a decade, people from the outskirts of my life

who I didn't expect would give a shit
about me or my pain sent me kind messages.
Those who could not perform bare minimum sympathy
don't get to witness this vulnerability. It is reserved
for my friends. My proven friends.
No strangers, no proven strangers allowed.

Step 2: Accept help.

My best friends help me
cancel my wedding plans.

Bert and I were supposed to get married
eleven days from now.

Before my dad passed, I talked
to the social worker at the hospice
who spoke with the building director and general manager.
They both gave me the green light
to hold the wedding at the hospice building
so that my dad could be there
even if he attended in his hospital bed.

When I told my dad about these plans, he told me

I'll try to be there.

I hope he did not worry about disappointing me
as he was trying to breathe.

I hope
                    I hope
                                        I hope

I didn't tell him we planned to cancel the wedding
if he passed away. I didn't want him to feel guilty

for being sick.

I can't have a wedding when I don't have bones,
when I don't have nerves or synapses or blood.
I can't marry a person if I'm not even sure
if I was marrying them out of love or out of desperation
just to share a moment with my father.

Bert messages me saying he has a plane ticket on hold,
asks if I want him here. I tell him

Please come.

When he arrives the next day, I teeter in his arms
like I drank a bottle of chardonnay on my own.

I'm so happy you're here,
I say.

My throat rasps like I'm sick
with a winter cold.

He drives us from the airport
to my ~~parents'~~ mother's apartment.
He helps take care of the dogs,
he helps with the chores.
And we let him.
No one says,
Oh, you don't have to. It's fine.
He's surpassed the title of guest.
We just say *thank you.*
Because we need help.
We still need help.
I will need more help
in the near future. Help
finding a job. Finding
a place to live. Finding
meaning. Finding

joy.

And I will accept the help I'm offered.
From Bert.
From my friends.
From anyone.
Even strangers.
Even those I just cut out of my life.
I'll pull out the needle and thread, the super glue,
the tape, find a way to mend the pieces
if they reached out to say,

I'm so sorry for your loss.

Step 3: Gratitude.

It's hard to imagine I have anything to be grateful for
when I can't quite make it anywhere
without a pillow or blanket.

I crawl to the kitchen,
unable to stand upright.
I open the refrigerator door,
and close it without taking anything.

I crawl to the shower,
reach for the handle from the outside
of the tub. Sit, shoulders leaning
against the toilet. The water heats
but I turn it off before getting in, crawl back
to the dark room.

My hairbrush sits on the sink untouched.
My toothbrush sits on the sink untouched.
My clothes sit on my body untouched.
I sit untouched.

Day and night, my Logical and Emotional Minds
wage war against each other. I keep
wondering if there was something I could have done
differently the night he died, something
that would have helped him, something
that would have saved him.

Logical Mind knows that, of course,
I'm not a doctor. I don't have any medical training.
If I were a doctor, if I did have medical training,
it wouldn't have mattered: he had a Do Not Resuscitate order.
He didn't want to be saved.
He didn't want to be saved
just to continue his bedridden life.

Either he was going to die alone,
or he was going to die holding my hand.

And there's no world that exists
where I would choose differently.

I muster the gratitude. Force it into my mind from nothingness
like the first atoms that formed our universe as we know it.

I am grateful I had as much
time as I did with him. I am grateful
we loved each other. I am grateful
we ate a meal as a complete family. I am grateful
we each sat in a chair in a circle
around my dad's hospital bed
with plastic plates of food
provided by hospice in our laps. I am grateful
for the one moment
that everything
felt okay.

I am grateful for my dad's sense of humor,
for the love he showed my mom, myself,
anyone who came into his life.

I am grateful for the work I did in another life,
caring for adults with disabilities. In another life,
I bathed and diapered and spoon fed
those who needed it. Was trained to do that work.
Paid to do that work.
Like the nurses in hospice,
I could provide this care with kindness
until I moved on from that job onto another one,
leaving the people I cared for behind.

The training and experience I gained gave me
the knowledge and confidence to care for my dad
to the end of his life, gave him the confidence to let me.

He felt more comfortable having me help
him with his intimate needs than he would have felt
having the young women working at hospice help him.
These were nurses whose jobs it was to care for people,
but they were nonetheless
strangers.

I am grateful Bert and I haven't fought.
Though I don't have the strength
to eat a bagel, let alone fight
or care about anything enough
to fight about it.

I am grateful to be an abandoned
building, leveled to splintered boards
and wayward roof tiles. My pain is a testament
to the joy my father brought to my life.
Shortly before my dad's passing,

I was brought to tears by an interview
between Anderson Cooper and Stephen Colbert,
touched by the comedian's earnestness, the expression
I had never before seen on his face.

I never knew he lost his father as a young boy
along with two brothers
in a plane crash.

He said,
I want it to not have happened,
But if you are grateful for your life …
then you have to be grateful for all of it.
You can't pick and choose what you're grateful for…
What do you get from loss?
You get awareness of other people's loss,
which allows you to connect with that other person,
which allows you to love more deeply and to understand
what it's like to be a human being,
if it's true that all humans suffer.

The bell of truth tolled in my heart, rung
by his words. I am tethered to my friends
who I know have lost someone they love
by a rope I never knew even existed.

The rope even tethers me to people I once disliked:
a Tinder date who ghosted me,
a young woman who was clearly in love
with my ex, AJ, while he and I were dating.

I haven't spoken to either of them in over a year,
but I know both of them have lost
a parent; the invisible binds shackle us
to each other now, though they don't know it,
and I probably won't go out of my way to tell them.
The connection still persists.

I feel disconnected, too,
from the people who I know have not experienced
the exposed nerves of a close loved one yanked
by pliers from one's jaws.
I am different from them now. They can't know
the festering wound staining my teeth red, can't know
the taste of salt and iron in everything I eat.

I know because that once held true for me. I was the friend
who felt bad but who didn't know how terrible loss felt,
couldn't empathize like I can now.

But I'm still grateful for those friends
whose hearts hurt for me.
I'm grateful for all of the friends and acquaintances
who have gone out of their way to express their sympathy.
They are little bits of gauze soaking up the blood.

I have to keep repeating my gratitude,
clinging to it.
I am grateful I was there.
I am grateful he wasn't alone.
I am grateful we loved each other
so much.

I am grateful for Bert, for my true friends,
for my dog, for my sister.

> I am grateful, I am grateful, I am grateful.

Step 4: Maintain control.

I couldn't control my dad's cancer.
I couldn't control his death.
But I could control his tribute. I could honor him

with my eulogy. I practiced in the mirror
in my mother's bathroom and choked
through the first sentence the way my father choked
on his last breath. I read it over and over again
to myself. I practiced in the car as Bert drove us
to the church, chanting to myself

> *You need to be strong*
> *for eight minutes.*
> *Then you can crumble.*
> *Eight minutes.*
> *Be strong for*
> *eight minutes.*

I pictured myself standing,
shoulders back, chin up
in front of the attendees,
no quavering, no breaking.

> *Eight minutes.*
> *Eight minutes.*
> *Eight minutes.*

I spoke with eloquence
so that every word resonated, so that
everyone could hear about my father's life,
about what he meant to the world.
I'm proud I held it together to honor him well.
He would have been proud too, I know,
that I stayed strong for my mother.

Now, though, now
that the funeral is over
and my father is buried,
I'm having trouble
with this step.
In the midst of my father's illness,
I controlled my presence. I controlled my rage.
What do I have left to control now?

I spend days not eating,
then I eat
an entire can of Pringles in one sitting.
I spend days watching Netflix, playing Candy Crush
instead of looking for a new job or a new place to live.
I want to live
in sci-fi and rom-com worlds, worlds
made of chocolate bombs and sugar drops
matching in colored patterns. Away from here.

I walk the dog, resent her for needing me,
then love her for needing me, for loving me
even when I don't brush my hair,
or message someone back
or put a bra on. She loves me even though
I'm not looking for a new job
or a place for Bert and I to live.

I was sleeping on the floor when my mom walked in
with her Consumer Cellular flip phone and told me
she was talking to a bereavement counselor
and wanted me to set up an appointment.
I will, for her more than for me.
I can control that.

Step 5: Remember.

Lauren, my friend who lost her dad to pancreatic cancer,
once told me,
A day will come when you tell a story
about some completely insane thing
your dad used to do,
and you'll laugh
instead of cry.
What does that world look like?
The world where I don't unravel

every time I think of him.
Do cardinals visit front yards in this world?
Does the Big Dipper appear in the sky
between night time rain clouds?

What would it mean about me
to live in that world?
That I'm no longer grieving?
If I can laugh thinking about my father?
Would that mean he never meant
anything to me?
If I'm no longer affected by the bullet
lodged in my ribs?
What will it mean about me
as the daughter who cared for him
with her own hands?
What would remembering him
with joy instead of despair mean?
That I've grown used to his
absence?
I've become numb to
the father-sized hole in my heart?

In September, I couldn't imagine living
without my father. Couldn't imagine
what my life would look like
without him.

Now, I can't imagine remembering
my father without transforming
into a poltergeist haunting the poor
victims trying to live their lives
within my crypt.
I don't want to imagine.
Not because I enjoy the sadness
but because

his death deserves
to be mourned.

Step 6: Chaotically Repeat.

There's no end to Grief Road.
Instead of an exit ramp
onto a new highway or a cul-de-sac,
the road starts over again from the beginning.
It's not a loop, but a maze
without any street signs
to tell you where you will be next.

One moment you will be telling people
to fuck off and the next
you'll be accepting help from those same people.
You'll cling to gratitude, remember, then grasp
to maintain control over something inane
before telling someone
to fuck off again.

This is the road I will be riding on
for the indefinite future. But at least
there are other cars like mine winding their way
through the maze. I won't be alone in the confusion.

My father's death
is the worst thing that has ever happened in my life, yet
I will find gratitude for the fact that this suffering
has allowed me to love
and understand others more deeply. I will thank
all of the people who have stepped up
to give my car a jump, to change a tire, fill my tank,
or to just say, *You're navigating this hell hole so well.*
Because it all helps.

It all helps.

Step 1: Fuck off.
Step 2: Accept help.
Step 3: Gratitude.
Step 4: Maintain control.
Step 5: Remember.
Step 6: Chaotically repeat.

whole,

I am not a

only

disjointed pieces

held

together

the way

two

ventricles

taped to

an

aorta

won't beat.

Grieving

let me know the pieces butchered in front of you / the wild and gamey breath / the scent that blends into every shirt, every sheet / the shit not suitable for sensitive stomachs / censored in front of your mother / i want to choke on sobs born from someone else / i want to feast on your grief instead / to gorge on the pain you never dared to share with anyone else / the awful tastes / the sour flavor of violence / the muscle and sinew shredded by knife and fork / one slice at a time / i have practiced not looking away from the body brutalized / split open / i can smell the blood / and i'm hungry for the rot gaping from the marrow / for intestines unraveled at this table / let's share this meal together / let our flesh decay holding hands / let the crows fly away with our eyes

Let the Mice Run Away With Our Teeth

Grief is the Ghost

appearing from the earth
erratic breaths behind
my ear a reminder
of my errors and
my   errant   endeavors
grief is the   ghost
slithering in   my second
skin   refusing to shed
the   sibilant   specter seething
through its   scales   the   shadow
seizes   in the soot

grief   is the   ghost
foaming
at the   mouth   the phantom
aura   forging
through the
frothing   furrows
it's in my pillows
it's flailing in the feathers

grief   is   the ghost
that   still   haunts
my   house
my   living   house
oh   how it's
still
oh   how
it   lives

Haunted

I won't eat borscht. Not since— I used to savor
the earthy taste and smell, the color of beets. But
it spilled— It spilled from the ladle onto my hand

holding the ceramic bowl, cool— It was
November— Then the warm, the warm
red and the warm purple— On my hand—

No.   ***PleaseNo****. StopstopShhhh.*

   Stop.   *Please. It's okay.*

Shhhh.I'msorryI'm sorryI'm sorry. Please. I'msorryI'm

sorryI'm sorry.

Shhh.Shhhhh.Shhhhhh.   *PleaseStop.*

*PleaseNo.**No.No.No.** Please**. Shhhhhhhhhhhhhhhhh.*

Stopstopstop. ***StopPlease. Please. Please.***

It's okay.   ***No.** Shhhh.*

I'm sorry.

I'm sorry.

I'm —

The pot slept untouched in the fridge— Blue
sprouts climbed the glass lid. My partner—
He asked, *Do you want me to take care of it?*
and I— I said,
        Please.
                Sorry.

Protection from the Rain

The town was under siege by sniper fire,
I fled—a ghost, a nightmare—ashamed
of my own weakheartedness, for escaping

without the dog, twelve years old, eight teeth
missing, limped gait, the empty leash lifeless
behind her, lost amidst the hurricane of running

innocents. Pulsed with cowardice, my legs broke
for the lawn where you're buried. Even though
you are dead, even in my dreams, even though

your stone, flush with the grass brought
no cover from the metal rain, I still searched
for protection by your side. Lying crescent

around your grave, my hand stretched wide,
read the carved letters of your name. Face
in the dirt, I prayed for the dog to live,
bargained for her death to be quick.

The sage is burning but it's not enough
to quell these hauntings living in my drawers,
my closet, my nightstand. The smell
of decay overwhelming the halls, sleeps under
the bed. It crawls in the space between
the stove and the kitchen cabinets.
I wave the incense in the air, wild like
a maestro trying to control the phantoms of brass
and strings, but they hover over the bed off-beat,
seep into the upholstery off-key, throw
cymbals in the shower, leave piano strings
coiled on the stairs. They own this place,
this pit for ghosts, they wrote the notes,

They Keep the Score

Portrait, 2020

our father sits / on my shelf a
portrait on a prayer card
between two paper weight
giraffes / gilded memories of a
trip to the zoo a younger version
of himself once took with his
two daughters / one lies curled
on its side looking up into our
father's face / the other stands /
neck curved / bowed like the
heads of the dead sunflowers
that haven't been thrown away /
hunched sentinel behind him /
with their furled petals weeping
in silence one after the other.

Portrait, 2021

After *David St. John*

The radio keeps me up   listening to the country
songs that help me remember   I remember he asked
me how much of me was nature and how much
was nurture   How much I was willing to give
     How much I was willing to give
up   We all lionized him   acknowledged our help
-lessness as our king lost feeling   lost hope
     but never lost us

     His photo lives on my shelf in front of the same vase
of sunflowers that still stand dead behind him after
a year   I look at his face now from across the room
just like I did before the end   catalog each tooth
     each eyelash   like I might forget
     like I might write a poem
that wasn't about him   like I might hold onto a truth
outside of grief

     I stare at nothing I know his face is ink on paper
yet one eye is slightly bigger as it always had been
     and I remember   Willie Nelson quavers through the static
     and I remember
     I remember I'm in the first stage of mourning   writing
like I'm trying to prove I'm not lying   The lamp light gilds
the ink   and I remember he's still gone
     I remember he's only a portrait on a shelf
I remember he's only a portrait
in a poem   I remember   I remember

Catholicism Still Lingers
in a Concrete Poem

The organ's aria rang out from
the National Cathedral,
quivering free the most
delicate of the cherry blossom,
petals with its chords, littering
the sidewalks of Wisconsin
Avenue with belated valentines
as she took her dog out on
Easter Sunday morning alone,
too early to call anyone just to say hi, not even her devout, Catholic mother.
And this woman's lonely, atheist heart found itself brushing her hair for her,
covering her night-old eyeliner with a pair of glasses, pulling up stockings
underneath a floral dress and pink cardigan, walking her, as if on a leash,
the half mile to childhood familiarity in the shape of a pew and a hymnal. Is
it so surprising though? When her heart knew she needed something,
anything, even if it was only to admire Romanesque architecture and stained
glass? To fall trance to the hollow murmur of responsorial psalms? She, like
her mother, had held onto so much for so long without a place for it all to go

Hadn't she already spent a
year pretending untruths were
true for the sake of a quiet
pulse and six hours of sleep
each night? Hadn't she
already wished on side-walk
pennies, dandelion seeds,
birthday candles and stars,
and even nothing at all to
manifest her unrelenting
daydreams into reality? What
would one more try hurt?
What are prayers, anyway, if
they are not the release of our
desperate, captive hopes
into the wild?

Swan Song

Her wings cup,
bow as if

        resisting the lake
        where she seeks

reprieve, like she's
changed her mind,

            saw something she hadn't
            from the clouds, the way

      her feathers flail just
      before her toes settle

into the cold.
but she's firm

        in her choice.
        this is where

          she wants to be.
          the ending is only

    a chapter in her story.
    some believe a swan's

grace lies in her poise
on the water. It does,

        of course, but most have
        never considered her ability

  to recompose year after
    year after each fall.

Two Years Later

In the aftermath of my dad's death, I wrote
the final step to surviving tragedy was

Chaotically Repeat.

I believed once I merged onto this grief road,
there was no exit from the maze
of looping tarmac and infinite dashed lines.
I thought the road was the end.

I was incorrect.
The road is not the end.

I wrote that final step
two weeks after my father died.
The newly acute pain
blocked any imagination
of feeling anything
other than slashed,
like a century-old tarp
weathering a hurricane.

I couldn't imagine a life
in which I could think about my dad
and not feel the shards of my glass shell
plummet to the ground in spiny fractals.

Even though I was told
by those who have traveled this highway before me
that I would learn to carry this pain,
that the weight would lessen over time,
I didn't believe them.

I was different, after all.

My relationship with my father was different.
I would carry this flesh-crushing weight forever.

And I do.
I still carry this heaviness.
I cry as I write these words, as I think
about how I have not spoken to him, hugged him,
or heard him laugh in two years.

It will only be longer and longer still.
Three years, Four. Ten years, twenty.
The time passes.
Not like a bolt of lightning
but not like a tortoise either.
It just passes.

My cry has became a soft cry—a pillow
rather than a wrecking ball.

I can hold the glass shards in place,
live with their jagged incompleteness.

Before and after my father passed away, my mind fixated
on W.S. Merwin's poem "Separation."
Everything I did was stitched with the color
of my father's death. I couldn't see or feel anything
other than this shadow.
I didn't want to.
I was not open to life, love, healing,
not open to laughter, forward movement, joy.

Being anything other than a breathing corpse
felt like a betrayal to my father's life, like I was hiding
my pain or, worse, not feeling pain at all.

But with time, therapy, and poetry, the pain now lives

woven in a tapestry of other emotions; it is no longer
the only thread. My world is now stitched
in variegated tones.

I've lived to see the other side
of Step 6, even though I did not realize
when I wrote the steps that there'd ever be
a new chapter in my life beyond them.

Grief Road, I've discovered, is not
just swerving among lanes
on an endless loop of asphalt.

> The end of Grief Road is
> healing.

It seems intuitive, but, in fact, it is not. While I existed
in the eye of grief, I never thought I would describe myself as

> healed.

I suppose I still don't. *Healed* sounds so
> finite,
as if a balloon archway and red and gold banner
beam the word FINISH into the distance
with a giant stopwatch marking the time it took
for me to cross over into the land of the healed,
crowds on either side cheering with dollar-store
poster boards, announcing,

> *You did it!*
> *You're healed!*
> *This way to the beer tent.*

I can say instead that *I am more healed,*
that I will continue to be more and more healed
as my life continues. More healed so that I can

laugh at a joke, or even tell one. More healed
so that I could possibly be disappointed,
or even disappoint someone.

The mind has to do what it needs to
to survive, after all.

I am out of the eye, I am more healed.
I can remember loss
without telling people to fuck off.
I can be grateful
without needing to cling to gratitude.
I can accept help
while not being helpless.
I no longer need to grasp onto control
as a distraction from my helplessness.
I can remember,
without falling apart.

But I was right that
I'm not alone in the confusion.
I never was, never will be, although—

Bert and I didn't get married.
Not even later on. Instead,

we returned to Wyoming
and moved into a one-bedroom apartment,
where we struggled.

A lot.

I quiet quit my life,
doing only the bare minimum
to not be fired
from my job,
from my relationship,
from my friendships.

My only interests were my dog, poetry,
and rice pudding with chocolate chips in it.

Bert struggled to be my hero
the way he imagined being my hero.

He did swoop in for me when I was in distress
as if standing akimbo, cape fluttering in the wind
behind his perfectly groomed beard.

But when I began to emerge from my own tomb,
the one in which I buried the woman
who once had a mother and a father,
when I looked at life again,
accepted my new role in the universe,
I didn't need him to be my hero.

With time and (lots of) therapy, I emerged
from the dark infinity that was so easy to succumb to.
A day would pass where I thought about my dad,
talked about him, looked at his picture
without collapsing into a pile of worms.

As I healed, I just needed Bert to be
my partner,
but we never quite figured out
what an everyday, boring life
together
looked like.

It was never *bad*. But
even from the beginning,
my relationship with Bert only worked
when he needed to rescue me
from a warehouse full of bombs,
or unshackle me from the ocean rocks

just before the tide came in.

Maybe when we first dated,
before my father's diagnosis,
when I pulled away, complained
that he bought me flowers too often,
maybe I felt as if he were trying to rescue me
when I didn't want to be rescued.

Being the youngest in the family, feeling
as if I had three parents, instead of only two,
I've resisted people doting on me, feeling
as if they see me as incompetent, that they need
to take care of me because I can't.

When I fell into the infinite abyss, I did need
to be taken care of because I could not care
for myself. I needed him to drive me
and my dog across the country, to fly back and forth
from Wyoming to Florida, to marry me within months
of knowing me, to hold my hand behind my dad's casket,
to cradle me even as I dry heaved
from the severity of my sobs.

When I texted him that September asking
if he would sit with me while I sobbed, maybe
I was drawn to his need to rescue instead of to *him*.

Over time, as I crawled out of it, elbow by elbow,
I didn't need and didn't want his doting anymore.

Maybe he felt like I was ripping
the cape from his shoulders. Or maybe,
he started to heal too.
Maybe he took his cape off himself.

He dismissed me unless I was having a meltdown.

He didn't understand why I kept having meltdowns.
We struggled to compromise when our wants lived
on opposite sides of the world. Every (dis)agreement ended
in lose-lose.

After spending a year and a half of a
not-unhappy-but-not-really-happy life
together, our lease term came up for renewal,
and it felt like with our apartment, the lease term
on our relationship came up for renewal as well.
He didn't want to sign.

Both relieved and bitter, I knew I didn't want to marry
the wrong person, but I also didn't want to start over.
I was willing to live with good enough.

Bert was stable, reliable, put-together, and trustworthy—
qualities I would not have attributed
to any of my previous exes.
I was okay having a good enough life together
when all of my former relationships weren't good
enough in the first place.

Good enough was not good enough for Bert, though.

He moved out of our apartment.
I followed suit a couple months later.

In hindsight, it is easy to see
it was just easier to have consistency and security
rather than having to embark on the journey of dating again,
easier to accept I would exist in a laughless marriage
because I knew the dishes would always be clean
and the dog would always be walked and the showerhead
would never be caked over with lime, and when I came home
from working a twelve-hour shift, there'd be a decaf coffee
waiting for me on the counter.

I didn't want to be 34,
wanting kids,
having to start over.

I probably would not start over with one person right away.
There'd be the excess of Tinder matches
who would be perfectly... fine who I'd have to meet first
before I met someone who would do all the cooking,
dance with me in the kitchen to Bobby Womack,
who would make brilliantly bad puns, do all the vacuuming
because I hate the sound of the vacuum, someone who would kiss
my neck and send an electric current through my skin.

We'd have to meet each other's families, have our first fight,
decide to move in together, decorate,
learn the ins and outs of one another's bodies and lives,
love those ins and outs,
learn each other's imperfections,
love those imperfections.
We'd have to do each other's laundry,
learn each other's love languages.
It'd all have to be perfect, or
at least, good, and not just good enough,
before we'd decided
we wanted to bring
another human into this world together.

Why go through all of that
to risk not finding anyone?
I rather have 50% of what I want
Right now and forever guaranteed,
than give it all up
for the chance of someday having 100%
when I could just as easily wind up
with nothing
and no one.

I can't hold it against him
For not feeling the same way.
Besides maybe I was even less-than-half
of what he wanted.

In the end, we still respect one another.
I never wondered where he was
or who he was out with.
We never called each other names.
I never feared him, even when he was angry.
I never worried he would lose control.
He never stared at other women while we were out.
I never had to pick up after him.
I never had to pick him up
because he was too drunk to drive home.

We just weren't great together.
Instead of peanut butter and jelly,
we were peanut butter and pizza.
Great separately. Maybe not so great as a pairing.

So now, we're friends.

And that's perfectly okay.
I am perfectly okay.

I have found a new life purpose.
A friend, who also lost her father to cancer, and I
not only bonded over our fathers dying,
but also over finding healing from loss
through poetry.

I am grateful for our newfound closeness,
for the new life I now have as a result of poetry—
a life I never imagined, a life
where, like my friend Lauren prophesied,
I can remember that time my dad left my mother horrified

after he ate a ramekin of butter at a nice restaurant
just because I dared him to, and I can laugh about it.

In a way, my dad lives on
through my poems,
through these poems, and if there *is*
a balloon archway with a red and gold banner
with HEALED blazoned across it,
these poems inch me closer
one stanza, one line, one word at a time.

Gloria Steinem said,
> *The final stage of healing*
> *Is using what happens to you*
> *to help other people.*
> > *That is healing in itself.*

Now that I am overlooking the valley
from the summit of Mount Grief,
I understand why so many people reached out
to help in the beginning. Their help was a manifestation
of their own healing. Help, it turns out,
heals both the helper and the helped.

Now I feel like I can navigate other cars
on this highway, like the driver whose job
it is to navigate traffic through a construction zone.
I write about this grief,
I speak about this grief,
I make art about this grief.

Being able to find
meaning from the worst thing
that ever happened in my life
lets me know

                    I am surviving now.

I'm no longer floating
with my chin above water hoping
a great white ends my misery.

I wouldn't even say I'm simply treading water.
I'm swimming.
I'm swimming and enjoying each stroke forward.

Whatever my curiosities are, I follow them,
then figure out how I will use my curiosities
to help other people.

It doesn't numb the pain into oblivion,
but it helps me feel like I can keep walking
on this path of life, that my legs are no longer
cement pillars.

It helps me feel like I'm honoring my dad
without letting myself slip through
the quicksand of grief.

And on some days,
when my heart is open to it,
it even brings me

joy.

Step 1: Fuck off.
Step 2: Accept help.
Step 3: Gratitude.
Step 4: Maintain control.
Step 5: Remember.
Step 6: Chaotically repeat.
Step 7: Find meaning.

I knew I'd never
see my father again after he died.
But I asked him every night he spent in
his hospice bed to please haunt me or send me
signs from the other side. I didn't realize he was
waiting for me on the moon. When I flew there in
a hot-air balloon one night, he stood smiling, full
-bodied, when I opened the hatch. We bounded
together, weightless, marveling at our bare
feet caked in gray dust. I woke to the
sound of my own laughter,
grateful I figured
out how to

meet
him

Halfway

Acknowledgments

THANK YOU

To my parents, the kindest, most loving people I have yet to meet. I am beyond lucky to have been raised by two human beings who taught me through their living example what true love looks like.

To my sister, my best friend, who never hesitated to be a sounding board for my poetry, this collection, and a million other things.

To Adanna Moriarty for introducing me to and insisting I apply to the Community Literature Initiative, for sharing your journey of grief with me, for healing with me side by side.

To Hiram Sims, Tommy Domino, Andy Sanchez, Alex Petunia, Ravina Wadhwani, and the entire Community Literature Initiative and Sims Library of Poetry teams for giving me the opportunity and support to build this collection. This collection would not have existed without you.

To early readers of this collection who provided feedback on many of these poems including Natalie Dunsmuir, Marissa Forbes, Christian Perfas, Evan Cummings, Jasmine Banks, Lolo Wink, Karo Ska, Brenda Vaca, and others.

Special shout out to my student and teaching assistant, Larissa Freitas, who calls me her "poetry guru," but who is really *my* poetry guru and whose insights truly made this collection what it is.

To Danielle Mitchell and The Poetry Lab team for providing a creative space to nurture my craft and be among like-minded artists. Creativity begets creativity.

To Shelly Holder for inviting me into her 30 for 30 class in a time when I needed it the most.

To Amanda Eke, Kristin Abraham, Aaron Wallace, Téa Mutonji, Nanci Turner Steveson, Noah Arhm Choi, torrin a. greathouse, I.S. Jones, and Natalie Eilbert, my teachers and mentors who helped me develop my craft.

To David Romtvedt, Juan Morales, Jonathan Fink, Matt Daly, and Laurie Kutchins for in-depth critique and feedback on many poems that made it into this collection.

To Connie Weineke of Jackson Hole Writers for hosting the monthly poetry group whose feedback contributed to many pieces in this collection.

To *Passengers Journal, Room Magazine,* Wyoming Arts Council, and Brooklyn Poets for providing support that led to pieces in this collection.

To Ravven White and Curious Corvid Publishing for believing in this collection and for believing in me as a poet. I am eternally grateful to you for giving me my first full-length manuscript in print.

To Anjelica Singer, Yuya Kiuchi, Emily Stirr Hager, Kayla Maryles, Lauren Pollow, Jessie Watsabaugh, Robert Moreno, and Alex Hart for believing in me.

To Matt Stech for being the love of my life.

To the following publications who first published some of the poems in this collection, sometimes in previous iterations.

"Am I still…" *Passengers Journal*, 2020.
"The Bridge to Empathy" formerly titled "Enemy Bridge." *Muddy River Poetry Review*, 2020.
"Catholicism Still Lingers in a Concrete Poem," *SixFold,* 2022.
"Elegy," *Anansi Writers Archive,* 2021.
"Eta Ursae Majoris" formerly titled "From Relative to Ancestor." *Passengers Journal*, 2020.
"Eta Canis Minoris," *Platform Review,* 2022.
"Gravestone Flowers," *SixFold,* 2022.
"Grief is the Ghost." *Brain Mill Press*, 2021.
"Grieving." *Meniscus Literary Journal*, 2020.
"Halfway." *Turbulence & Coffee,* 2021.
"I Now Know." Passengers Journal, 2020.
"I Will Remember You This Way," formerly titled "Shell." *In Parentheses*, 2020.
"Let the Mice Run Away With Our Teeth," *SixFold,* 2021.

"Make a Wish, Darling." *Variant Literature*, 2020.

"Meager Material," formerly titled "Inadequate Materials." *Courtship of the Winds*, 2023.

"Portrait, 2020." *SixFold,* 2021.

"Remains of a Man" formerly titled "Remains." *Santa Fe Writers Project,* 2021.

"Sepsis" formerly titled "Prayers." *In Parentheses*, 2020.

"Stone-faced." *Unlimited Literature*, 2020.

"Waves Away." *Alchemy Literary Journal*, 2020.

About the Poet

Anne Marie Wells (she | they) is an award-winning Queer poet, playwright, memoirist, and storyteller navigating the world with a chronic illness. She earned the Peter K. Hixson Award in poetry through Writer's Relief and the Milestone Award through Wyoming Writers Inc. She was nominated for Wyoming Woman of Influence in the arts category for amplifying the voices of LGBTQ and disabled communities in Wyoming through her writing. She is the lead faculty member for the Community Literature Initiative DC Chapter and strategic partnership fellow for The Poetry Lab.

Find her online at
AnneMarieWellsWriter.com
or @AnneMarieWellsWriter

www.ingramcontent.com/pod-product-compliance
Lightning Source LLC
Chambersburg PA
CBHW051005140626
46546CB00016B/507